A CULTURE OF SILENCE

THE STORY OF FOOTBALL'S BATTLE WITH HOMOPHOBIA

BY

JASON MITCHELL

Copyright © 2012 Jason Mitchell & JMitchell Media, UK.

ISBN: 978-1-291-01210-1
Publisher: Lulu

All rights reserved. Written permission must be secured from the author to use or reproduce any part of this book, except brief quotations in critical reviews and articles.

The opinions expressed in this book are those of the author of this book and do not necessarily reflect the views of the publisher or its affiliates, or any of the companies and organisations mentioned within.

JMitchell Media: http://jmitchellmedia.wordpress.com

Contents:

Introduction	5
Institutionalised Homophobia	11
The Tragic Story of Justin Fashanu	25
Players Views on Homosexuality Within Football	43
Silenced By Supporters?	55
Homosexuality in Other Sports	65
The Role of the Media	77
A Glimmer of Hope	83
Back to Reality	89
Homophobia in Women's Football	95
Promoting Homosexuality in Football	101
Conclusions	107
Bibliography	115

Introduction:

As a heterosexual football fan, my first-hand experience of homophobia within the sport is somewhat limited. That said, when attending live football matches, in various stadiums across the United Kingdom, I have witnessed homophobic abuse from supporters, aimed both at rival fans and players. In my experience, it is not at all uncommon to hear players being subjected to homophobic taunts from the terraces, often based on their appearance, the fashion accessories they choose to wear, or their behaviour on the pitch. Several players also have to endure abuse stemming from rumours in tabloid newspapers about their sexuality, or as a result of club rivalries. Words like "faggot", "poof" and "queer" are commonplace at many football grounds and most supporters probably hear them on a regular basis, to the point where it might not even fully register in their minds as being abuse or discrimination. That does not, however, make it an acceptable part of the sport.

According to research carried out by Stonewall, three out of five lesbian, gay or bisexual football fans believe that football is an anti-gay sport. Around half of gay supporters admit that their own participation in the sport, both in terms of playing the game and attending live matches, has been affected by football's inability to tackle anti-gay abuse.

While playing football at school during my childhood and playing with my friends in my adult life, I have also witnessed similar anti-gay remarks being made to people, often because they look a certain way or they do not, for some reason, live up to a certain masculine stereotype associated with football.

Obviously, it would be wrong to suggest that football is the cause of all of this homophobic feeling; I have, after all, witnessed homophobic abuse in other areas of life, completely away from the context of football and, sadly, I am sure many of those who give out such abuse at football matches carry similar views into the rest of their lives. However, in my experience, something about football as a sport does seem to intensify the problem. Perhaps, within football, homophobia is thought of as being more socially acceptable than it is elsewhere.

One of the most worrying things about the homophobic abuse I have witnessed inside football stadiums is the fact that, at present, no professional players in the United Kingdom, or indeed in any other top football leagues, are actually openly gay. Despite the statistical inevitability that there are gay footballers out there, all of them have chosen, for reasons that will be explored in this book, to remain silent about their sexuality. For the most part, victims of homophobic abuse in the game are just perceived as having gay characteristics for some reason, or the supporters have chosen to utilise homophobic slurs as a generic way to insult them. It does, however, beg the question: what sort of abuse would a top level, openly gay player have to endure from these same fans, if he chose to reveal his sexuality?

Although I have personally witnessed homophobia in football grounds, those experiences were not my primary motivation for writing this book. In actual fact, one of my biggest motivations was the story of Justin Fashanu, a player who died in 1998, having previously been the first - and to date, only - openly gay player to play professional football in the UK. I was inspired by his bravery, appalled by the abuse he was subjected to for revealing his sexuality and saddened by the circumstances surrounding his tragic death. Upon researching his story in more detail, I was also shocked by the extent to which football, as a sport, had failed Justin Fashanu, as a human being. It amazed me that some highly respected figures within the game had completely turned their backs on him in the aftermath of his revelation, yet they faced very little in the way of repercussions for their actions, while Fashanu's life spiralled out of all control.

Despite my own experiences with homophobic abuse, I have been fortunate enough to be born into an era where society, at least in my home country of the United Kingdom, is probably more tolerant than ever before. Racism is far less of a problem than it was even twenty years ago, and homosexuality is generally accepted by most people. Of course, discrimination still exists, but many of the worst stories of discrimination in modern history took place before my lifetime. What struck me about Fashanu's story, in particular, was the fact that it happened so recently.

On closer examination, I soon discovered that Fashanu was far from alone in his experience within the sport. Indeed, many other players have been subjected to similar homophobic abuse and many other respected figures in the game have engaged in anti-gay discrimination. In some ways, football can, therefore, be seen to be lagging behind the rest of society; as if it is stuck in some bygone era, when homosexuality was still a taboo subject.

After discussing the issue with a few of the people close to me, it became apparent to me that many football fans are also completely unaware of the extent to which homophobia exists within professional football. Although there have been television documentaries about the topic and newspaper articles covering specific incidents, generally, it remains an under-reported area of the sport; especially in comparison to other social issues, like racism and sexism.

As I began to dig deeper, I became interested in some of the debates that surround the subject. Have lessons been learned since Fashanu's death? Can open homosexuality ever exist in football? Why does open homosexuality even need to exist? What makes football different from the multiple other professional team sports, which have embraced the presence of homosexual athletes? Is football an anti-gay sport? I decided that these questions, Fashanu's story and other, similar stories would make for a compelling book; a book about football's baffling inability to accept homosexuality.

Football is one of my biggest passions in life and this book is not really intended as an outright assault on the sport as a whole. For the sake of clarity, this book is also not aiming to publicly 'out' any current professional footballers as being gay. It is, instead, intended to expand public awareness of the type of homophobic feeling which still sadly exists inside football, in an effort to hopefully work towards changing it. This book will analyse homophobia in the sport, assess exactly who or what is to blame for the lack of openly gay players and examine potential ways to solve the problem. It will also assess the cultural issues caused by the lack of a clear homosexual presence within the sport, especially in terms of the lack of gay role models for homosexual youth to look up to, and the limited depiction of homosexuality they are presented with.

This book is motivated by the need for tolerance and acceptance of homosexuality in football, and by the need for gay footballers to be able to exercise their right to a free choice over whether they express their sexual preference. It is time for football to make steps towards breaking the taboo, changing attitudes and creating an environment where it is both safe and acceptable for a gay footballer to publicly acknowledge his sexuality, if he so chooses. As this book will hopefully demonstrate, the key problem at the moment is that that environment of choice simply does not exist.

Football has created a culture of silence amongst the homosexual athletes in the sport. It is time that steps were taken to enable them to break that silence.

Chapter One:
Institutionalised Homophobia

In 1998, Justin Fashanu, the world's first openly gay professional footballer, took his own life in tragic circumstances. In the aftermath of Fashanu's death, and as attitudes within society as a whole have changed, issues surrounding homosexuality and homophobia in football have emerged as a talking point within sections of the media and in the sport itself. More specifically, a focus has been placed on the lack of openly gay, male professional footballers who are currently active in the sport. In addition, clubs, players, governing bodies, the media and supporters have faced increased scrutiny for the way they approach the topic of homosexuality within the game.

In 2005, while researching the implications of the Civil Partnerships Act, HM Treasury and the Department of Trade and Industry concluded that 6% of the population of the United Kingdom should be classed as gay; one in every 16.6 people and an estimated 3.5 million people in total. As of 2012, there are over 4,000 professional footballers playing the game in England alone. Despite this, there are currently no openly gay professional footballers in the country and there have not been any since Fashanu. If football were to follow the trend of the general population exactly, there would be around 240 active gay footballers in England today. Deviation from the figures associated with the general population can potentially be explained by any number of different factors but, even allowing for extreme deviation, it seems incredibly unlikely that there is not a single gay professional footballer amongst the thousands of footballers active in England. This lack of homosexual representation within the sport becomes even more difficult to explain when you consider the fact that there are no openly gay footballers amongst the thousands of professionals playing in Scotland, Wales and Northern Ireland either. In a country where homosexuality is, for the most part, accepted as being a normal part of life, it seems incredibly strange that the nation's most popular sport has a complete lack of gay participation at professional level.

However, to suggest that this issue is exclusive to professional football within the United Kingdom would be drastically wide of the mark. In actual fact, this complete lack of openly gay professional players can be observed throughout all of the top professional football leagues across the world. In fact, with the exception two footballers far away from the mainstream - Swedish fourth division player Anton Hysén and American footballer David Testo, who, prior to announcing his sexuality to the world in 2011, was released by Canadian club Montreal Impact - at the time of writing this book, there are currently no active, openly gay professional footballers anywhere on the planet.

There are a number of different contributing factors to this lack of an open, homosexual presence within football; many of which will be explored throughout this book. One of those factors is the behaviour of people in high-profile positions of authority within the game. Over the years, several major footballing authority figures across the globe have made statements, in which they have suggested that any gay footballers out there should remain discreet about their sexuality, either for the sake of their own career or for the sake of others.

In 2011, the President of the Italian Football Association, Damiano Tommasi, explained his own views on the topic. "Homosexuality in football is still taboo," he said. "In this sport the players practically live with each other. It's different to every other profession. Expressing your sexual preferences is difficult in all environments, even more so for a player who shares the locker room, which is an intimate space, with others." Tommasi went on to advise against gay footballers making their sexuality publicly known, or even known to their team mates. "I wouldn't recommend coming out," he said. "I don't think one needs to talk about his sexual preferences in order to work or live in a civil environment. Personally, I have never known gay football players. Maybe I did and just didn't realise they were homosexual."

Tommasi's view that football is different from every other profession in the world can, of course, be considered massively blinkered. Other professional sports, which also operate on a team basis, with players sharing changing rooms and spending large amounts of time together, have coped perfectly well with the presence of homosexual athletes. Tommasi seems to be suggesting that homosexuality and football cannot co-exist, which is a very damaging attitude for someone in such an important position within Italian football to have. Unfortunately, this is fairly typical of the sort of attitude within football that has been described by some critics, including the gay rights group Stonewall, as "institutionalised homophobia."

It also appears that Tommasi's issue is not necessarily a personal agenda against homosexuality itself, but instead a belief that homosexuality within football could cause heterosexual people in the sport to feel uncomfortable in their place of work. This viewpoint would be completely unacceptable from an authority figure in almost any other profession. Perhaps, in this regard, Tommasi's claim that football is different from every other profession has an element of truth to it. As such, he claims homosexuality is a 'taboo' within the game, seemingly accepts that status without question, yet doesn't actually produce a valid reason for why that should be the case. However, in the face of such advice from the President of the country's FA, it is no surprise to learn that Italy has never housed a single openly gay professional footballer.

These views are not limited to Football Associations and, in fact, are present amongst many other figures of authority working in the sport. Luiz Felipe Scolari, a former World Cup winning manager with Brazil, and one of the most widely-respected men in the game, has also been accused of harbouring homophobic views. During his time as Brazil manager, in 2002, he was quoted as saying, "If I found out one of my players was gay, I would throw him off the team." In the aftermath of his comments, Scolari rejected accusations he was homophobic. "My friends include people whose sexual preference is different from my own," he said. A classic defence, but let's just assume for a moment that there is an element of truth to that claim. Like with Damiano Tommasi, it appears there is a divide between Scolari's personal feelings on homosexuality in wider society and his views on homosexuality within football. He finds the former acceptable and the latter unacceptable, yet, once again, it remains unclear why he feels the presence of a gay footballer would be so troubling. Obviously, any gay footballer in the country will have seen or heard Scolari's comments and taken heed. In such a climate, it is virtually impossible for open homosexuality to exist. Why would a gay player in Brazil even entertain the idea of coming out publicly, when such an important footballing figure has already stated he would kick them off his team if he found out about their sexual orientation? Clearly, in that situation, for any Brazilian player with ambitions of representing his national team, coming out as gay would only hurt their own career.

Some authority figures in continental Europe have publicly expressed even more extreme and openly homophobic views than Scolari's. In November 2010, Vlatko Marković, the President of the Croatian Football Federation, was quoted as saying that he did not believe that gay footballers should be eligible to play for the Croatian national team. "As long as I'm president there will be no gay players," Marković said. "Thank goodness only healthy people play football." Unlike Scolari, Marković made no attempt to distance himself from accusations of homophobia, and this grossly offensive view, characterising gay people as being in some way abnormal, should have received widespread condemnation from within the country and, indeed, from others around the world. Instead, it was publicly defended by Zdravko Mamić, the executive vice president of top Croatian football team, Dinamo Zagreb. Mamić decided to add his own brand of bigotry to the debate, telling daily newspaper 24 Sata: "I would not have gay people playing in my national team either. Gay people are for ballet." Once more, it seems obvious that no gay footballer would dare to express his sexuality in such an obviously hostile environment.

Although the United Kingdom generally plays host to less openly hostile attitudes towards homosexuality in football, as a country, it has proven itself to be no more capable of tackling homophobia within the sport than Italy, Brazil or Croatia. In 2005, BBC Radio Five Live reporter Matt Williams contacted all of the active football managers in the Premier League, asking them a series of questions as part of an investigation into homosexuality in football. He intended to find out why the managers felt there were no openly gay professional players in the league, whether they believed an openly gay player could fit into the dressing room culture of the sport and whether or not they felt homophobia was a topic that football needed to address. Every single one of the managers refused to respond to the questions.

According to Williams, some of the managers or club representatives claimed that the questions made them feel uncomfortable, while others explained that they did not participate in questionnaires or surveys. Yet, despite these objections, all twenty of the managers responded to questions from the same reporter about security in football grounds, during a separate investigation. In a revealing twist, in response to his investigation into homosexuality, Williams received an email from one club, which contained a response intended to be sent internally, rather than to Williams. It stated "Should we touch this or palm it off with a 'can't comment'?" It is therefore clear that homosexuality, as a subject, is considered to be off-limits, even at the biggest and most respected football clubs in England. This is a tremendous shame, as intelligent, influential and respected men like Jose Mourinho, Sir Alex Ferguson and Arsene Wenger would likely be able to have a huge influence in the battle against homophobic discrimination in the sport, if only they were willing to speak out against it. Instead, it seems most managers and clubs would rather 'palm it off', bury their heads in the sand and pretend that homosexuality does not exist in football.

The 'don't ask, don't tell' attitude that many within football have adopted towards dealing with the issue of homosexuality is clearly not helpful and surely goes a long way towards explaining the lack of openly gay players. Gay players likely feel they have little choice but to accept it. While that approach may work to avoid uncomfortable changing room situations, it does absolutely nothing to tackle football's general inability to accept homosexuality as a normal part of society. The fact is, homosexuality exists and there is absolutely nothing to be gained from pretending it doesn't.

Football is a game which, over the years, has provided careers to people from all kinds of backgrounds, including violent criminals, convicted rapists and other sexual offenders. It is a sport which has embraced footballers with questionable political views, footballers with substance abuse issues and even a few footballers who have killed other human beings through their own reckless actions. FIFA, the sport's global governing body, openly promotes the sport as being an inclusive and unifying influence in the world. Given those facts, it remains difficult to understand why, of all things, homosexuality is considered by so many to be professional football's last remaining taboo.

It is also fair to say that football's inability to deal with homosexuality extends beyond being an issue with gay professional players. In 1987, FIFA reacted with outrage when referee John Blankenstein was supposedly spotted wearing FIFA-branded clothing in a gay bar in Canada. Blankenstein, who sadly died from a kidney disease in 2006, was notable for being one of the first athletes to come out as gay in the Netherlands. "They said it didn't matter that I was gay. But to be seen in a FIFA suit in gay surroundings? That was unacceptable," Blankenstein explained. In actual fact, Blankenstein denied being in the bar in the first place, but dealt with the outrage by turning the focus back on FIFA. "Who was the FIFA representative who recognised me [in the gay bar]?" he asked. He received no response.

Blankenstein also believes that being gay cost him in terms of his career. He has stated a belief that his sexual orientation was the reason he was not given the opportunity to referee at the 1990 FIFA World Cup. Additionally, in 1994, when Blankenstein was selected by the European football governing body, UEFA, to referee the Champions League Final between Barcelona and AC Milan, his sexuality likely played a role in the opportunity being taken away from him.

In Italy, Blankenstein's appointment as the senior match official was met with a strong negative reaction, partly due to his nationality. As a Dutchman, it was believed he could be biased towards Barcelona, who, at that time, were managed by Johan Cruyff; quite possibly the greatest Dutch player of all time. However, his sexuality was also seized upon by the Italian media as a reason for why he should not referee the match. As a result, Blankenstein received death threats from sections of the Milan support and was eventually replaced by Philip Don as the referee for the match. The official line from UEFA was that Blankenstein was replaced for safety reasons, although he expressed a belief that his sexuality was the real reason, as authorities felt his sexuality was bringing too much negative publicity to the event.

Prior to his death, Blankenstein also revealed that he personally knew of at least five gay players in the Dutch league, some of whom, he claimed, were living alibi lives, in heterosexual marriages, as a way of maintaining their careers. Despite not naming any names, this revelation added more credibility to the argument that there are gay players out there, but they feel they need to maintain a heterosexual public image for the sake of their careers.

Blankenstein, who campaigned strongly against homophobic discrimination in football, died believing that one day open homosexuality would be possible and acceptable in the sport he loved.

Sepp Blatter, President of FIFA, also caused controversy with his own insensitive behaviour in the build up to the 2010 FIFA World Cup, by talking about the issue of homosexual supporters. When asked whether cultural issues surrounding homosexuality in Qatar would create problems for gay fans going to the 2022 FIFA World Cup, the first to be hosted in the middle-east, Blatter, apparently joking, replied, "I'd say they [gay fans] should refrain from any sexual activities." The response was met with laughter from those in attendance, before Blatter chose to follow up with a more serious answer, stating that he believed there would be no problem. Blatter was subsequently criticised for the tone of his initial response and the message it sent out to others in and around the game, regarding the topic of homosexuality in football.

This response, and the laughter which followed, is fairly typical of the 'boys club' type of atmosphere which exists within professional football. Perhaps it is easier to make a joke about a difficult cultural situation rather than face up to a real issue or perhaps many of those involved in the game have very immature views on the subject. Regardless, Blatter and FIFA also came under criticism from several high profile figures, including former NBA star John Amaechi, for the decision to host the 2022 World Cup in Qatar in the first place. Those objections were mostly based on Qatar's general intolerance towards homosexuality within society. "It's not about people having sex in public and being sanctioned for it," Amaechi explained. "It's the fact that Qatar was one of 79 countries to sanction executing gays at the United Nations." Probably not the best location to host a sporting tournament then; especially one which invites thousands of supporters from all across the world, bringing together various different cultures under FIFA's banner.

There is an argument to say that FIFA do not, and should not, have the power to change the culture of the countries which choose to make bids to host a football tournament. Let's be clear; Qatar's internal, social issues with homosexuality are not the fault of FIFA and not really for football to deal with. Interestingly enough though, FIFA took a much more hard-line approach to dealing with another, seemingly less serious cultural problem in Brazil, ahead of the 2014 World Cup. Alcoholic drinks are banned in football stadiums in Brazil, a decision that authorities within the country made in 2003, in order to cut down on increasing incidents of violence at football matches. This did not sit well with FIFA executives, especially given the fact that they have a lucrative sponsorship deal with Budweiser. In response to the ban, FIFA General Secretary Jerome Valcke stated, "Alcoholic drinks are part of the FIFA World Cup, so we are going to have them. Excuse me if I sound a bit arrogant but that's something we won't negotiate." It therefore seems that FIFA are perfectly willing to exercise the huge amount of power they possess to place political pressure on countries to change their laws and customs - but only if there is a commercial interest for them in doing so. Is the consumption of alcohol by supporters a more important issue than gay rights? No. Is it more financially rewarding for FIFA? Yes. And on such criteria are decisions made.

Perhaps the most frustrating thing about homophobic feeling existing within the sport's governing bodies and football associations is the fact that these huge organisations have almost unlimited financial resources at their disposal to attempt to tackle the problem and make a real difference. The anti-racism campaigns they have spear-headed are admirable and have helped the sport to take huge steps forward in terms of race relations. Although racism has not been eliminated entirely, and likely never will be, those within the sport who engage in racist behaviour are generally met with harsh punishments and, above all, there is a clear message from FIFA, UEFA and the various football associations that such behaviour is unacceptable. If the same emphasis was placed on eliminating homophobia within football, it is likely that similar long-term progress could be made. The problem is that punishments for homophobia remain inconsistent and are sometimes even non-existent, and campaigns against homophobia remain relatively low-profile by comparison, partly because the people in charge struggle to even understand the problem and, even more amazingly, some of them are entirely complicit in it.

As conversation about the lack of openly gay footballers has become more common, a counter-argument has developed to the idea that gay players should be able to express their sexuality openly and honestly. In short, the argument states that there is no major issue regarding the lack of openly gay players in the sport, because the personal lives of footballers should be of no concern to the general public, or indeed the media. It is not newsworthy for a footballer to be heterosexual, so why should it be newsworthy for them to be homosexual? While it is true that footballers should be perfectly entitled to keep their private lives private and gay people are perfectly able to be proud of their sexuality without publicly flaunting it, this viewpoint remains flawed for several reasons.

Hypothetically, if a footballer is gay and genuinely wishes for that information to be kept away from public knowledge, for their own personal reasons, then there should be absolutely no issue with that. In fact, very few people would argue that a homosexual footballer should be *forced* to come out publicly. The issue lies squarely in the fact that at the moment football does not provide an environment which presents the decision to come out as a realistic choice. The homophobic feeling which exists in the sport makes it almost impossible for a gay footballer to publicly acknowledge their homosexuality, because they are encouraged, by authority figures within the sport, to avoid doing so. A homosexual footballer is made to understand, in no uncertain terms, that revealing their sexuality could be detrimental to their career. So, in light of that information, why would they want to reveal it? The fact that coming out as gay in the twenty-first century is accepted so willingly as being career suicide is, frankly, ludicrous.

In addition, the opportunity to speak openly about their sexuality could serve to liberate some homosexual players, both on and off the field, and also allow them to have a positive influence on young gay men and women, many of whom may wish to pursue careers in sport, but feel unable.

Britain's foremost public relations advisor, Max Clifford told British newspaper The Independent in 2009 that he had personally represented two top-level gay professional footballers in England over the last fifteen years. Despite this, Clifford says that he cannot envision a gay footballer publicly coming out in the near future. "If he did, it would effectively be his career over, in my view," he told the newspaper. "Do I think that's right? Of course not. It's a very sad state of affairs. But it's a fact that homophobia in football is as strong now as it was ten years ago." Clifford advised both of the gay footballers he represented to remain secretive about their sexuality. As such, as a public relations advisor who works externally from the sport, he was right to do so. Clifford does not possess the power to change football's homophobia problem by himself. Within the existing culture, his advice was good advice, for the sake of the players' livelihood. Obviously, that should not be the case, but unfortunately it is.

Meanwhile, Peter Clayton, who heads up the English FA's 'Homophobia In Football' working group, claims that there are gay footballers in England who have expressed their sexuality openly within their clubs, but have chosen to keep that information away from the media. "There are gay players in the top division in English football, and some of them are out to their clubs and team mates and nobody gives a jot," he said. Clayton himself is a pioneer within the sport, as he is the FA's only openly gay councillor. If what he says is true, it suggests that fellow professional footballers are able to take a more mature approach to the topic of homosexuality than many of the people in control of the game. However, there have also been many documented instances of footballers displaying homophobic attitudes in recent times, and these will be examined in more detail later in the book.

Additionally, despite Clayton's presence within the organisation, the English Football Association has come under fire for being behind the times in terms of how it treats the subject of homosexuality. For its part, the FA repeatedly reasserts its "commitment" to eradicating homophobia in football. However, Ben Summerskill, the chief executive of Stonewall, believes that one of the biggest issues is the association's inability to admit to their problems. "The FA has been in denial at a senior level, and until recently they did not acknowledge that there was any serious problem," he said in 2010. He also believes that football should look to the armed forces, another occupation that has, over the years, been plagued with homophobic attitudes, for advice on how to tackle the subject. "We're sending openly gay and lesbian people to fight in Afghanistan, but we can't send openly gay people to fight for the World Cup. The chiefs and generals in the armed services understand that people perform better when they can be themselves at work – you feel more comfortable and are more productive – and that will be true of professional football, when it finally happens, as well."

Chapter Two:
The Tragic Story of Justin Fashanu

"I wanted to do something positive...so I decided to set an example and come out in the papers." These are the words of Justin Fashanu, written in the book 'Stonewall 25', discussing his decision to publicly acknowledge his sexuality in 1990. Fashanu was the world's first openly gay professional footballer. His talents on the football field, as a powerful centre-forward, also led to him being the first black footballer to transfer clubs for £1 million; but it is the former fact which dominates his legacy.

In truth, Justin Fashanu lived a somewhat troubled life from the very beginning. At the age of four, his biological parents split up and he and John, his younger brother, were sent to live in an orphanage. When Justin was six the two brothers were adopted by white, middle-class foster parents, Alf and Betty Jackson, and spent the duration of their childhood in Shropham, Norfolk, a predominantly white village. The two brothers were virtually inseparable during these early years, having already experienced their fair share of misfortune and suffering together.

Although raised in a loving environment, the racial divide in his family and in the community meant that Justin Fashanu grew up confused about his identity. Some of his neighbours from the time have claimed that he desperately wanted to be white and would never openly refer to himself as being black. During his youth,

Justin also experienced traumatic and terrifying nightmares and would often sit up in the middle of the night and react violently to them. On one occasion, at the age of around 15, he woke from a nightmare and punched through his bedroom window, shattering the glass in the process. These nightmares would continue to haunt him throughout his adult life. With the benefit of hindsight, it is easy to see how some of the psychological issues which manifested in Fashanu's life could have been formed during his childhood.

Throughout his teenage years, Justin Fashanu excelled at various sports. He displayed a real talent for boxing and seriously considered it as a career prior to eventually settling on professional football.

A product of the Norwich City youth team, which he had joined at the age of 14, Justin Fashanu signed his first professional contract in December 1978 and made his league debut against West Bromwich Albion on 13 January, 1979. Upon his arrival in the first team, Fashanu, an articulate and seemingly confident young man, quickly established himself with his powerful displays and his goal-scoring ability. In total Fashanu scored 35 goals in 90 league matches for Norwich; a very good record, especially given the Canaries' position in the league table during those years. One goal in particular would catapult Fashanu to national fame.

In February 1980, at the age of just 18, Fashanu scored a truly spectacular goal against Liverpool, announcing himself on the national stage in the process. The ball arrived to Fashanu, who had his back to goal, on the edge of the box. A more experienced player may well have laid the ball off to a team-mate, but Fashanu, fuelled by the confidence and imagination of youth, flicked the ball up, turned and volleyed it into the far top corner, much to the amazement of everyone watching. To score such a goal against any level of opposition would be impressive, but the goal was made even more amazing by the fact that it was scored against the reigning league champions. As a result, the goal was replayed on television countless times and was later crowned the 'Goal of the Season' by BBC's Match of the Day. It brought Fashanu new-found media attention and would become the defining moment of Justin Fashanu's playing career. His performances for Norwich City, including one dominant display against Nottingham Forest, eventually caught the attention of Peter Taylor, who, in turn, recommended him to Brian Clough. Clough decided to make Justin Fashanu, now 20-years-old, his replacement for Trevor Francis, who moved from Nottingham Forest to Manchester City.

In August 1981, Fashanu completed his trail-blazing £1 million move to Nottingham Forest. Fashanu, who had by this point featured in the England B team, seemed at surface level like a perfect fit, and Brian Clough, in those initial stages, even predicted that the other teams in the league would be "petrified" of his new star signing. Unfortunately, what should have been an exciting new chapter in Fashanu's young career would instead end up being one of the most difficult periods of his entire life, as he struggled both personally and professionally.

Brian Clough was one of English football's best-loved characters and one of the country's best ever managers. After applying for the England national team job on various occasions, and being unsuccessful, he became known as 'the greatest manager England never had'. In the years prior to Fashanu's arrival, Clough had steered Nottingham Forest to a league title and two successive European Cups; a period of dominance that had not been seen before at the club, and has not been seen since. Although a hugely successful manager, his training methods were, at times, unconventional. One of his former players, Viv Anderson, once told a story of how Clough had his players run through stinging nettles in an effort to psychologically mould them to obey his every command. "We did it without question," Anderson said. Clough ruled with an iron fist, operated a regime where his word was law and generated a culture of fear at the club. He would openly bully some of his players in a bid to get the best out of them and, make no mistake about it, for many of them, it worked wonders. However, Fashanu was still a raw talent and a fragile young man. His apparent self-confidence was little more than a façade, which hid a vulnerable player who needed to be nurtured more carefully than some of the other players Clough was used to dealing with.

In one of his first training sessions at Nottingham Forest, Fashanu, eager to impress his new manager with his ability, ran over to take a corner kick. Instead, far from being impressed, Brian Clough barked at Fashanu in anger. "I didn't pay £1 million for you to take corners, now get in the box!" Clough, an old-fashioned manager very much set in his ways, struggled to grasp Fashanu's soft-spoken nature, his personality and his fashion sense and regularly criticised him for all three. This style of management was unlike anything Justin Fashanu had experienced at Norwich and a personality clash between Fashanu and Clough soon became apparent.

Around the same time, to make matters worse, Fashanu was slowly coming to terms with his own sexuality. Although he had been aware of homosexual feelings during his days at Norwich, it was not until after his move to Nottingham that he fully realised that he was gay. He soon began to live a closeted double-life, attempting to hold his own in the macho world of professional football, while privately living out a lifestyle which included frequent parties and visits to gay night-clubs. Although Fashanu was not open about his sexuality at this stage, Brian Clough had received phone-calls making him aware of these night-club visits and had come to suspect that Fashanu, the big and powerful centre-forward he had paid £1 million for, was in fact gay. The idea of a homosexual footballer was certainly not something which appealed to Clough, who had always expected his players to adhere to a stereotype of ultra-masculinity.

In his autobiography, Clough described a subsequent dressing-down he gave to Fashanu. "Where do you go if you want a load of bread?" Clough asked. "A baker's, I suppose," came the reply from his centre-forward. "Where do you go if you want a leg of lamb?" "A butcher's," Fashanu answered. "So why do you keep going to that bloody poofs' club in town?" Clough was proud of this story and often retold it, feeling that he had made his point effectively.

Fashanu was no stranger to discrimination in football. Throughout the 1980s, racism was commonplace in English football and he had already suffered abuse from supporters, many of whom had directed monkey chants towards him and some of whom had even thrown banana skins onto the pitch. But, although he tried to laugh it off, it was the rejection from his manager, the great Brian Clough, which hurt and disappointed Fashanu the most. "Clough doesn't respect or support me," he confided in his close friend, Peter Tatchell on several occasions. Fashanu, still a young man, needed Clough's support and, so far, he had seen no sign of it.

In a desperate bid to get his manager's approval, Fashanu lied about being engaged to a woman. Clough subsequently arranged a dinner where he intended to meet the woman, feeling it was an important part of his job as a manager to know and understand the private lives of his players. He soon realised that the beautiful young woman who arrived on Fashanu's arm was not his real fiancé, or even a real girlfriend. "It was all a con, a charade, or at least that's what I believed and still do. It was Fashanu's way of trying to convince me he wasn't gay," Clough wrote in his book. Clough now saw Fashanu as a liar and a fraud, as well as a homosexual. In reality, Fashanu was simply not ready to publicly acknowledge his sexuality yet and did not want to be treated differently from other players by his manager. He tried to conform to the stereotype Clough expected, but his failure to accept himself for who he really was only served to make an even bigger enemy out of his manager. It seemed like Fashanu could not win.

During his time at Nottingham Forest, Fashanu had also embraced evangelical Christianity in an effort to make sense of his personal struggles. Although he eventually failed to make his faith and his sexuality co-exist, partly due to his church damning homosexuality and making him feel uncomfortable and ashamed, his attempts to do so also angered Clough. "Found God?" Clough asked. "Good. I should get him to sign a few cheques for you," he said sarcastically. It seemed that, by this point, just about everything Fashanu did angered Clough in some way.

The relationship between the two rapidly went from bad to worse. On more than one occasion, Fashanu broke down in tears after speaking to his manager. This display of open weakness also did little to impress his manager. Clough would regularly refer to Fashanu as a "poof" and at times even resorted to using violence against him. Once, when Fashanu pulled out of a game prior to kick-off because he felt he was not fit to play, Clough lashed out and hit Fashanu on the side of the head. On another occasion, Fashanu turned up to training with a friend, identified by Clough as being either his personal masseur or religious teacher. Clough, who by his own admission could stand no more of him by this point, demanded that Fashanu leave the training ground immediately. Fashanu, finally having been pushed over the edge, refused and a stand-off followed. It seemed their relationship had reached boiling point. Clough, who was aware of Fashanu's boxing background and was unwilling to get into a physical altercation, through fear of being embarrassed in front of his players, called the police and asked them to escort Fashanu away. After the police arrived, Clough, who now felt he was safe from any retaliation, kicked Fashanu in the calf and told him to get off the training ground and out of the club. "He was weeping buckets," Clough recalled, proudly.

It is no surprise that in such an unstable environment, Justin Fashanu completely failed to live up to his £1 million price tag. He scored just three goals in thirty-two league games for Nottingham Forest, putting in some dreadful performances along the way. Clough later described the £1 million transfer fee as "the worst money we ever invested" and after thirteen months at Nottingham Forest, he was loaned out to Southampton. At Southampton, Fashanu's career briefly picked up again and he scored three goals in nine games for the club; a decent record. Southampton manager Lawrie McMenemy wanted to sign Fashanu on a permanent basis, but financial limitations at the club prevented him from doing so. Instead, in December 1982, Clough sold his £1 million signing to rivals Notts County, for a mere £150,000.

"He used to burst into tears if I said hello to him," Clough later said of his relationship with Fashanu. "Here was a slip of a lad, twenty-one or so, who had so many personal problems that a platoon of agony aunts couldn't have sorted him out. Hey, I'm a football manager, not a shrink. I couldn't talk to him, 'cause I didn't know what I could say that would make any difference."

Although Justin was considered by many in the sport to be the more talented brother, it was brother John Fashanu who went on to achieve real success in football, winning the FA Cup with Wimbledon in 1988 and representing England on two occasions. At Notts County, Justin scored 20 league goals in 64 matches before moving on to Brighton & Hove Albion for £115,000 in June 1985. During his time at Brighton, Fashanu's knee was punctured by an opponent's stud. At the time, the injury looked to have robbed him of his career for good.

Fashanu, unwilling to give up on his career, flew out to the United States to have surgery on his knee and eventually, in 1988, after extensive rehabilitation, returned to playing football, first for Los Angeles Heat in the U.S. and later for the Edmonton Brickmen and the Hamilton Steelers in Canada. His form at Edmonton, where he scored seventeen goals in twenty-six league games, went some way towards encouraging Fashanu to try to rejuvenate his football career in England.

On 23 October, 1989, Fashanu joined Manchester City and played two matches in the first division, failing to score in either of them. Less than a month later, on 20 November, he moved to London to join up with West Ham United and played two matches for them, again failing to score on either occasion. At this point, due to his previous knee injury, Fashanu was advised that it would be extremely difficult for a club to get insurance for him. As a result, he struggled to find a permanent employer. A trial at Ipswich Town also failed to land Fashanu a contract before, finally, in March 1990, he joined Leyton Orient.

During his time at the East London club, Fashanu, for the first time, began to seriously consider publicly announcing his sexuality. Not having done so already was beginning to take a toll on him privately, as he felt as if he wasn't being totally honest with himself or with those around him; like he was living a lie every time he stepped onto a football pitch. He spoke at length to his manager, Frank Clark, who actually advised Justin that coming out as gay might not be such a bad idea. Clark suggested that doing so could help to take the pressure off him and allow him to focus on football. Justin, however, was understandably terrified of how he would be treated by people in and around the game. At that time, he eventually decided against coming out. "He was adamant that he wasn't ready," Clark explained.

Fashanu soon changed his mind, partly due to a tragic loss in his life. A 17-year-old friend of his, who had been kicked out of his house by homophobic parents, had taken his own life as a result of the rejection he had experienced. Distressed by the news, Fashanu decided he wanted to act as a role model and to make a change, so that he could help to prevent other young men from making the same choice. "I felt angry at the waste of his life and guilty because I had not been able to help him," Fashanu said of the incident.

Propelled by an eagerness to prevent similar tragedies from happening, as well as his own internal identity crisis, the decision was made and Fashanu sold his 'coming out' story to The Sun newspaper, the biggest daily newspaper in the UK. On 22 October, 1990 they ran with a front page headline: '£1m Football Star: I Am Gay'. Fashanu coming out was national news.

The bravery of Fashanu's decision to be the first professional footballer in the world to come out as gay should not be downplayed. It was an even braver decision when you also consider the lack of openly gay black men in the public eye and the fact that he chose a tabloid newspaper, with huge distribution, as the place to make his revelation. Although some dismissed the move as a cynical money-making attempt to help pay the debts he had acquired from his knee injury and subsequent surgery, it is no exaggeration to say that Fashanu's decision to come out publicly, in such a strong way, broke down cultural barriers, even if those barriers have seemingly been rebuilt in the years that followed. Coming out was also a decision made at great potential risk to his career and life. Fashanu would later go on to explain that the decision to choose a tabloid newspaper as the place for his revelation was partially motivated by this risk. "I genuinely believed that if I came out in the worst newspapers and remained strong and positive about being gay, there would be nothing more they could say," Fashanu explained. "Unfortunately I was wrong."

Many figures from within the game spoke out against Fashanu's decision, with some claiming outright that homosexuality had no place in the sport. In turn, Fashanu took the criticism well. "You have to understand," he calmly explained, "that footballers are very narrow-minded people. When you put yourself in the firing line, you are open to attack. I know I'm there to be shot down in flames." In the face of adversity, Fashanu seemed to be coping remarkably well.

However, one of the most vocal critics was his own brother. A week after The Sun's exclusive with Justin Fashanu, The Voice newspaper, primarily aimed at a black audience, printed an exclusive interview with his brother John, under the headline: 'John Fashanu: My Gay Brother Is An Outcast'. Once united by their shared childhood struggles, John effectively disowned Justin. In another interview, Fashanu stated: "I wouldn't like to play or even get changed in the same vicinity as him. That's just the way I feel. So if I'm like that, I'm sure all the rest of the footballers are like that." The two brothers would go on to have little or no contract during what would turn out to be the last years of Justin's life. John Fashanu felt embarrassed and humiliated by his brother and believed that Justin had brought shame upon their family. Like with Brian Clough ten years earlier, Justin once again found himself being shunned by someone who could and should have offered him public support in a time of need.

"It's disappointed me," Justin said of his brother's reaction. "I thought that he had more depth and more tolerance, because we've been through so much together, especially as kids. I think it has disappointed me because I thought he was better than that."

Justin Fashanu tried to re-ignite his football career after coming out. Although fully fit once again, he still struggled to find a team willing to offer him a full time contract. After a failed trial at Newcastle United in October 1991, he eventually signed for Torquay United a month later. Fashanu was unable to prevent the club from suffering relegation and suffered constant homophobic abuse from supporters. Again though, for the most part, Fashanu seemed to cope well with the challenges presented to him. On one occasion, supporters chanted abuse and Fashanu simply wiggled provocatively, in a tongue-in-cheek response. During another match a supporter engaged in homophobic and racial chanting and threw a banana onto the pitch. Fashanu, feeling it was best to tackle the abuse head-on, simply ate the banana. In yet another football stadium, while once again being victimised for his sexuality by supporters, he simply blew kisses to the section of the crowd who were abusing him. In truth, far from struggling, a certain part of Justin Fashanu actually seemed to relish the controversy and the attention. Despite being thought of by many as a side-show attraction, mostly due to his sexuality and domination of headlines, his performances on the football field for Torquay were actually quite impressive. Fashanu scored ten goals in twenty-one games for the club.

Fashanu also claims that his fellow professionals at Torquay were mostly accepting of his sexuality, despite occasional malicious jokes. However, Fashanu's behaviour was becoming more and more erratic. Around the same time, he generated newspaper headlines for a supposed relationship with former Coronation Street actress Julie Goodyear. It seemed as if, by now, he was becoming addicted to publicity and scandal, played out in front of a national audience through the tabloids.

In February 1992, Fashanu became assistant manager of Torquay and a year later he made a failed attempt to take over as manager. He left the club soon after the disappointment. Short spells at Airdrie in Scotland and Trelleborg in Sweden followed, before Fashanu joined Hearts in July 1993. Early in 1994 his contract with the Scottish club was terminated for 'unprofessional conduct'. By this point in his career, Fashanu had a complicated relationship with the national media and the termination of his contract was fuelled by the fact that he had attempted to sell false allegations to the press about supposed homosexual relationships he had had with Conservative MPs.

Following the sacking at Hearts, Justin Fashanu was clinging to his playing career by a thread. He soon returned to the United States, joining Atlanta Ruckus in 1995 before moving to New Zealand to play for semi-professional team Miramar Rangers in 1997. Later, he moved back to the U.S. once again after being considered for a coaching role at the newly formed team Maryland Mania. No contract was officially signed, but it is believed he was the prime candidate for the job.

While in Maryland, in March 1998, Fashanu was accused of sexually assaulting a 17-year-old boy. Fashanu, who had developed a popularity in the area through his natural charm, hosted a party at his flat one night. Several other teenagers, both male and female, were in attendance, as Fashanu had apparently been reaching out the local youth, hoping to generate interest in his new football club. The 17-year-old, named in subsequent newspaper reports as 'DJ', was a fair-haired boy, with a weight-lifters physique, who could reportedly bench-press 200 pounds. DJ was enjoying the party but soon became involved in an argument with his mother over the phone. Apparently, the argument was over what time his mother wanted DJ to be home by. After hanging up and continuing the party, DJ eventually asked Fashanu if he could stay there for the night. "I'm too drunk to go home," he said. Fashanu obliged.

Around 2 a.m. that night, according to DJ's claims, Fashanu raped him. DJ reported the incident to his mother early the next morning and she, in turn, reported Fashanu to the police. When police questioned Fashanu over the incident a short time later, he remained remarkably calm, answering all of their questions and even agreeing to take a polygraph test in order to clear his name. Fashanu claimed the allegations were nothing more than an extortion attempt; that the boy had found out he was rich, had demanded money during his stay at Fashanu's house, and that Fashanu had refused to pay. According to Fashanu, the rape allegations were an attempt to force Fashanu's hand.

The police investigation eventually concluded that Fashanu had indeed engaged in anal sex with the boy, although it could not be concluded at that time whether or not the sex was consensual. However, reports emerged that police had returned to Fashanu's flat in Maryland, intending to arrest him on charges of first-degree assault, second-degree assault and second-degree sexual assault. By then, Fashanu had already boarded a flight and returned to England.

On 1 May, 1998, Justin Fashanu made a phone call to his brother John. When John answered, Justin did not speak. John heard breathing on the other end and claims he immediately knew it was Justin. Rather than reach out to his brother, he instead hung up the phone. On 2 May, 1998, Justin was spotted visiting a gay sauna. Later on the same day, apparently believing that there was a warrant out for his arrest and with nowhere to turn after the rejection from his family, he hanged himself in a deserted lock-up garage, in Shoreditch, London.

In one of his final acts, Fashanu wrote a suicide note in which he once again protested his innocence. He wrote: "I want to say I didn't sexually assault the young boy. He willingly had sex with me and then the next day asked for money. When I said no, he said 'you wait and see.' If that's the case, I hear you say, why did I run? Well, justice isn't always fair. I felt I wouldn't get a fair trial because of my homosexuality." Fashanu also stated that his decision to end his own life was motivated by a desire to spare the feelings of his loved ones. "I realised that I had already been presumed guilty. I do not want to give any more embarrassment to my family," he explained.

An inquiry into Fashanu's death later revealed that there was no warrant out for Fashanu's arrest, although reports vary on the reason why. Some claim that police would have made an extradition request but they were unaware that he was in England at the time. Other reports suggest that the charges were actually going to be dropped completely, due to lack of evidence.

It would be entirely too simple to conclude that Justin Fashanu committed suicide as a result of being a gay footballer. In truth,

Fashanu was a deeply troubled young man; a man who had struggled with emotional problems throughout his life and who had been caught up in terrible accusations about his sexual conduct in his final months. However, it is clear that his career as a footballer suffered as a result of his sexuality, firstly under the management of Brian Clough, then as a result of abuse received from supporters. Through the words in his suicide note, especially his references to being "abandoned", it is also clear that the rejection he experienced from his family and friends for publicly coming out had contributed to his feelings of isolation.

An inquest into his death ruled that the homophobia he had to face up to likely played a part in causing him to be overwhelmed, especially when he became subject to a police investigation. It was in this overwhelmed state, with seemingly nowhere to turn, that Fashanu made his decision to take his own life.

Fashanu's experience in the game and subsequent suicide has an obvious effect on the current culture of silence surrounding homosexuality in football. Any gay footballer out there would have understandable reservations about coming out, through a fear of suffering the same hostility and experiencing the same fate. It sets a worrying precedent, and is an inescapable fact, that the only gay mainstream footballer to ever come out suffered abuse and rejection and eventually felt so hopeless that he took his own life. It is easy, therefore, to see Fashanu's story as a warning to other gay players that it is better to keep quiet than to open up about their sexuality.

Having said that, Fashanu's life should not necessarily serve to discourage gay footballers from making their sexuality known in the future. It is extremely doubtful that Fashanu would want that to be his legacy on the game and it needs to be made clear that his life was complicated far beyond simply being homosexual. In truth, people within the game have held Fashanu up as an example of why gay footballers should remain closeted far too often. At times, it seems it has even been used by those in the sport who harbour homophobic feelings as an excuse to discourage open homosexuality.

There are lessons to be learned from Fashanu's story, but, primarily, his story should be used as a driving force for change. The desire for what Fashanu experienced to never be repeated should act as a catalyst for increased tolerance of homosexuality, instead of the current silence which surrounds the subject.

In the years after his death, many within the game have shared their thoughts about Justin Fashanu's story. In his second autobiography, published in 2004, Brian Clough confronted the way he mistreated Fashanu, in an effort to make peace with himself. "When you hear of a lad taking his own life in squalid circumstances like that, a lad you once worked with and were responsible for, you have to look back and wonder if you could have done things differently," he wrote. "I know now that I should have dealt with Fashanu differently, certainly with a little more compassion and understanding."

On the other hand, his brother John Fashanu still struggles to deal with the issue. In January 2012, BBC Three aired a one-off documentary, entitled 'Britain's Gay Footballers', presented by John's daughter and Justin's niece, Amal Fashanu. In the documentary, apparently disappointed in him, John's daughter confronted him about his treatment of Justin. John told his daughter: "I'm not homophobic and I never have been, but at the time I was certainly cross with my brother. I sleep at night wondering all the time 'could I have done more?' and I keep coming up with the answer, 'yes, I could have done more'. Does that console me? No. We've cried for nearly two decades for Justin, it's enough." Yet later in the same documentary, John still refused to accept Justin's sexuality, concluding: "Justin wasn't really gay, he just wanted attention."

John Fashanu's present-day refusal to accept that his brother was gay is symptomatic of football's problem with homosexuality in general. It remains a sport which would rather pretend that homosexuality does not exist, instead of facing up to the problems created by accepting it – but homosexuality is very much a part of life and it needs to be accepted as a part of football.

Justin Fashanu's legacy is dominated by the fact that he was the first openly gay professional footballer in the world and by the fact that he eventually took his own life. Lost in amongst that is the fact that he was a talented footballer who broke new ground with his move to Nottingham Forest and was a player who had the talent to go further in the game than he eventually did. He was also a charismatic and intelligent young man who could have had a lot to offer the sport and the world in later life.

Regardless of the allegations surrounding him at the time of his death, the validity of which will now likely never be known for sure, Justin Fashanu is a man who has huge cultural significance. In a sport where it is deemed unacceptable to be different, Fashanu *was* different. On top of that, he had the courage to stand up and admit that fact. He was different and proud. For that reason, Justin Fashanu can rightly be considered a sporting hero.

While Fashanu's experience in the game acts as a warning for any homosexual players out there about the consequences of being open with their sexuality, it also simultaneously influences movements towards the acceptance of homosexuality in football. To some, Fashanu is a symbol of why open homosexuality cannot exist in the sport. To others, he is an inspirational figure, who gives hope that one day open homosexuality can exist within the game. In 2012, as part of her BBC investigation, Amal Fashanu stated, "I'm proud Justin was my uncle and that he was brave enough to say what he did. The game needs more people like my uncle if homophobic barriers are to be removed."

Chapter Three:
Player's Views on Homosexuality Within Football

Discussions about homophobia within football are often centred around the behaviour of those in charge of the game, in particular, football associations, governing bodies and football managers. However, it is vital to also examine attitudes towards homosexuality at the level where it can perhaps be most damaging; inside the changing room. Homophobic feeling in the sport has proven to be a difficult subject to tackle, partly because of the reluctance that many players have in discussing the issue. Campaigns aiming to eliminate anti-gay abuse in football stadiums have, historically, struggled to gain backing from high-profile players. It has been suggested that this reluctance stems from fears that they will be forever associated with homosexuality in the aftermath. In addition, some professional players have engaged in anti-gay abuse themselves. It could be argued, therefore, that professional footballers have played a role in keeping gay players in the closet. However, in light of Peter Clayton's claims that there are gay footballers in England who are open about their sexuality within their clubs, it is also important to also assess his idea that, perhaps, most professional footballers are not complicit in the homophobic feeling that exists within the modern game.

It is fair to say that, in support of Clayton's views, when discussing the subject of homosexuality within the game, some professional players have displayed a level of maturity far greater than that of many authority figures in the sport, even dating back as far as Justin Fashanu's playing career. Although Fashanu was the victim of some homophobic abuse and discrimination from players on the training ground and in the dressing room, he also insisted that, for the most part, his team mates at Torquay United were supportive of him after he came out. Likewise, reports from his time in the United States, New Zealand and Canada, as well as in other clubs in the UK, seem to indicate the same pattern of acceptance, ruined only by a small-minded minority, which sadly included his own brother. In truth, the vast majority of homophobic feeling aimed at Fashanu from within the game did not come from his fellow professionals, but instead from the media, his club managers and from supporters, who aimed abuse at him from the stands.

In the modern game there are clear examples of professional players who have adopted a mature approach towards the topic of homosexuality when asked to discuss it. Swedish footballer Freddie Ljungberg, perhaps best-known for his time with Arsenal, has been at the centre of speculation about his sexuality for many years, as a result of his bachelor lifestyle, fashion sense, lucrative modelling contract with Calvin Klein and open love of musicals. In a game so rife with homophobic feeling, it is little wonder that such traits are ignorantly considered to be the tell-tale signs of homosexuality; clearly they are at odds with the ultra-masculine ideal that many expect of a professional footballer. In response to the rumours regarding his sexuality, Ljungberg, a man remarkably at ease with himself, actually admitted that he found the speculation flattering. "There's been a gay rumour for a long time," he told the New York Times. "I don't mind at all. I am proud of that. I love fashion and I think so many gay people have amazing style. So that is a compliment to me." Ljungberg's open embrace of gay rumours demonstrates his own liberal attitude, likely the result of his upbringing in Sweden. Interestingly, it also casts homosexuality in an overwhelmingly positive light; perhaps even portraying it as a desirable quality for a footballer. Few others within the game have displayed such an unflinching response to rumours of homosexuality, and Ljungberg's response to those rumours provides a welcome change from the established norm of footballers distancing themselves from any such talk as quickly as possible, in order to avoid damage to their career.

Meanwhile, former Manchester City and Newcastle United midfielder Joey Barton also demonstrated his more sensible side when discussing his own views on the subject of homosexuality in the game. During the creation of BBC's documentary 'Britain's Gay Footballers', presenter Amal Fashanu soon found that most professional footballers she contacted were completely unwilling to participate in any sort of open discussion about homosexuality in front of a camera. After trying, and failing, to secure interviews with a string of mainstream Premier League footballers, including Rio Ferdinand, Joe Hart, John Terry and Theo Walcott, she soon found that Barton was the only high-profile player willing to discuss the subject with her. Amal Fashanu subsequently explained her belief that the other players had refused to be interviewed out of fear; they felt that being featured on the program would link them to homosexuality in some lasting way once the cameras had stopped rolling and would, perhaps, even encourage homophobic abuse against them in the future.

When he was told about other footballers' reluctance to approach the subject, Barton, who has a homosexual uncle, remarked that he felt pity for those players and expressed his disappointment at the fact that they were "not big enough" to come and speak out in support of such an important issue. Barton also explained that "archaic figures" in the sport, including some managers, struggled to deal with the entire topic of homosexuality. Interestingly, he followed this up by providing a rare, optimistic viewpoint on the nature of homosexuality in the game. "There is no doubt in my mind that within the next ten years we will have an openly gay footballer," Barton said. Although few seem to share Barton's optimism, it was certainly a refreshing viewpoint to hear, especially from an active, heterosexual footballer, with knowledge of the atmosphere at a training ground and in the changing rooms.

In 2001, David Beckham appeared on the gay magazine "Attitude" and during an interview with the magazine, he admitted that sooner of later the divide between football and homosexuality would have to be broken down. It represented an astute PR move for Beckham, who later appeared outside London's G.A.Y night-club in order to make the most of his large gay fan base. In doing so, Beckham became one of very few footballers to openly embrace his homosexual fans and thank them for their support.

There is an argument, therefore, to suggest that some professional footballers are able to demonstrate compassion and understanding when dealing with the topic of homosexuality. Despite this, it is a harsh reality that many players, past and present, continue to openly display homophobic views, and homophobia is still relatively commonplace in football dressing rooms around the world. These views drastically limit the likelihood of a mainstream gay professional footballer being open about his sexuality, by creating a fear that he would be rejected by his own peers for doing so. In almost all walks of life, the acceptance and respect of your peers is vitally important for self-esteem and general happiness. Football is no different. Yet, there appears to be an underlying fear amongst the closeted homosexual players in the game that revealing their sexuality could cause them to lose that respect. A string of incidents over the years have only added to this fear.

Despite being married with children, former England international left-back Graeme Le Saux was often subjected to baseless homophobic taunting from his fellow players. Bizarrely, the speculation regarding his sexuality stemmed only from his university education, love of art and antiques, and his general unwillingness to participate in the drinking culture that existed at the time. Le Saux's pursuits in his spare time were considered to be at odds with what was expected from a footballer. The abuse he received from his colleagues was so severe that he considered quitting the sport entirely and dreaded going to training every morning. "I was like a bullied kid on his way to school to face his tormentors," he wrote in his autobiography.

The anti-gay abuse Le Saux endured was not confined to from within his own team and, in fact, reached boiling point during a competitive match between his club, Chelsea, and Liverpool, in February 1999. Le Saux became involved in a series of altercations with Liverpool striker Robbie Fowler over the course of the match. At one point, as Le Saux prepared to take a free kick, Fowler made an offensive, homophobic gesture towards Le Saux, bending over and pointing to his backside in order to taunt him. Le Saux subsequently refused to take the free kick and, despite the obvious abuse from Fowler, Le Saux was given a yellow card by the referee for time-wasting. Enraged by the lack of action taken by the match official, Le Saux later physically struck Robbie Fowler. As a result, Le Saux was charged with misconduct by the FA. This is a clear example of football's inability to deal effectively with homophobic taunting during a match. The fact that Le Saux is not actually gay is irrelevant. He was subjected to anti-gay taunting and it should have been dealt with instantly, in order to stamp it out. Instead, Le Saux was left to be abused, until he reached breaking point, at which time, having been offered absolutely no protection from the referee, he took matters into his own hands. Le Saux was, for all intents and purposes, punished because he was unwilling to accept being discriminated against in his place of work. The incident is a key example of what could happen if a player in the spotlight opened up about being gay.

In 2000, Eduardo Berizzo, a former international footballer for Argentina, launched into an astonishing homophobic tirade when describing his time playing for French club Marseille. "A bunch of faggots is what you have in French football," he announced. "There are so many homosexual players there; they always provoke you. They touch your thighs, your bum, to see if you give some kind of signal. I feel disgusted when a homosexual shares the same shower and stares at one's bum with desire, and even gets emotional when you are naked." Clearly, any gay player would feel uncomfortable to be playing at the same club as a footballer who is happy to publicly brand players as "faggots" and announce that homosexuality disgusts him.

Furthermore, in September 2006, during a match between Benfica and Manchester United in the Champions League, Paul Scholes was seen shouting the words "fucking poof" after being issued a yellow card by the referee. Again, he was not punished for the homophobic language. The incident sparked outrage from gay rights campaigner Peter Tatchell, who later asked questions of UEFA and the English FA's lack of action. "Homophobic abuse is no more acceptable than racism." he said. "It is shocking that the football authorities allowed Paul's bigoted remark to pass without taking any action. If he had made a racist remark, UEFA and the Football Association would have initiated immediate disciplinary proceedings. Why the double standards?"

Tatchell's assertion that the authorities would have taken a different course of action if Scholes had used a racial slur is demonstrably correct. For example, when Liverpool's Luis Suarez was perceived to have made racist remarks to Manchester United's Patrice Evra during the 2011-12 season, he was given an eight match ban, fined £40,000, criticised for "damaging the image of English football around the world" and the FA released a 115-page report on the incident. His reputation was tarnished, the incident was a major international news story and he was warned that repetition of the same abuse in the future could potentially lead to a permanent ban from the sport. There is definitely a double standard in the way in which racial abuse and homophobic abuse are punished. Exactly why this double standard exists is far less clear.

A week after the incident involving Scholes, his Manchester United and England team mate Rio Ferdinand also faced allegations of homophobia when, during a live interview, he called BBC Radio One DJ Chris Moyles a "faggot." Amidst the shocked reaction from within the studio, Ferdinand quickly apologised, stating, "I'm sorry, I'm sorry, I'm sorry. I'm not homophobic." Some people, in the aftermath, argued that Ferdinand made a simple slip of the tongue, while caught up in the moment, having been provoked by the DJ, and certainly that may well be the case. That said, it seems very unlikely that a player making a racial slur in the same circumstances would have avoided punishment.

Former Manchester United midfielder Raven Morrison also caused controversy when, in February 2012, he replied to a fan on Twitter, calling him, amongst other things, a "little faggot". A spokesman for the Justin Campaign, responding to the remarks, released a statement saying: "It is disappointing to hear that yet another professional footballer in England has used homophobic language." After pressure from the Justin Campaign, the FA eventually fined Morrison £7,000. In the same month, Premier League footballers Federico Macheda and Nile Ranger were also both charged by the FA after making homophobic remarks on their Twitter accounts. This attitude from players is hugely damaging to any attempts to challenge homophobia in football. Although the remarks were not aimed at a footballer, they demonstrate ignorance and would obviously serve to discourage a gay footballer from coming out publicly. While the FA charge at least represents a reaction from authorities towards the homophobic attitudes within the game, in reality a £7,000 fine is little more than a slap on the wrist for footballers earning in excess of that amount every single week. It is less than a quarter of the amount that Suarez was fined for racism and, to put it into further context, Danish striker Nicklas Bendtner was fined approximately ten times that amount for revealing a personal sponsor on his underwear during a goal celebration at Euro 2012. It seems absolutely farcical that personal sponsorship deals are considered a more serious issue to football authorities than homophobic slurs made by players on social networking sites.

Gay rights campaigners were once again angered by comments from a high-profile footballer during the 2012 European Championships. Italian journalist Alessandro Cecchi Paone released a book about homosexuality, in which he claimed that he knew of two gay players and one bisexual player within the country's national football team. At a press conference, Italian striker Antonio Cassano was asked for his views on the matter. "If I say what I really think, there's going to be chaos," Cassano said. "Fags in the national team? That's their problem. But I hope not." Cassano later apologised for his remarks. Chris Basiurski, chair of the Gay Football Supporters' Network, immediately questioned what action would be taken against Cassano. "We don't want any special treatment, but we would like the sanction to be the same as it would be for a player who made a racist comment," he stated. "An England captain [John Terry] lost his job for allegedly saying something [racist] and he is now going to be hauled before the courts. I would be amazed if that happened to this guy. People would say it would be an overreaction but I don't think it would be."

Basiurski also believes Cassano's behaviour proves that homophobic feeling is still as strong as ever in football. "Every time a footballer opens his mouth and makes a homophobic comment it means that I don't have to answer the question of whether or not homophobia still exists in football. It clearly does. You can see it regularly," he said. "It is amazing how often the issue comes up and I don't understand why straight footballers need to talk about this a hell of a lot more than anyone else. I don't get that and I never have. These comments seem to be coming all the time now and he is not the first person to say this sort of thing."

Cecchi Paone also spoke out against Cassano's reaction to his book. "Once the Euros are over, I invite Cassano to dinner so I can explain to him how wrong he is on this, because I think his ideas are a little confused," he said. "I want to help him understand that he was very rude to his team mates, who are forced to hide themselves. By being forced to hide, they cannot play their best football."

Cassano faced some short-lived outrage from certain sections of the media but, ultimately, he faced very little in terms of major repercussions for his remarks and went on to represent his country throughout the rest of the tournament, even playing in the final against Spain.

Former Republic of Ireland international Tony Cascarino has also been especially outspoken about how he believes a footballer would react towards a homosexual team mate. "Would a player mind if he found out a team-mate was gay? Probably," Cascarino said. "Players wouldn't want to be left alone with him, they wouldn't want to shower with him." In attempting to explain the psyche of the average professional footballer, Cascarino, perhaps unwittingly, seemed to reveal his own ignorance towards homosexuality. Yet, if he is correct about the response from professional footballers, it appears that a gay man in a football changing room would be treated more like a sexual predator than simply a person with a different sexual orientation.

When speaking of the homosexual players he had personally dealt with, Max Clifford explained his understanding that, in general, professional footballers have a complete inability to cope with the topic of homosexuality. Clifford believes that fellow professional footballers create one of the greatest obstacles for a gay footballer who wants to be open about his sexuality, and claims the players he has spoken to have expressed to him that homosexuality would be considered to be "totally unacceptable to the other players."

In addition to some of the outright homophobic views, other footballers have spoken out to advise players not to come out as being gay, citing concern for their well-being as the reason. German national team captain Philipp Lahm is one such player. Lahm wrote in his own book, "I would not advise any football player to come out. I would be afraid that something might happen to him, as it did to Justin Fashanu." Lahm's view is certainly not motivated by any discrimination towards homosexual footballers; on the contrary, it is a statement seemingly made with their best interests at heart. However, it displays a remarkable willingness to just accept homophobic feelings and attitudes within sport; a fact which is particularly disappointing given that Lahm, as the captain of his national team, has enough influence to instead challenge these attitudes. There is an argument to suggest that, instead of warning gay footballers not to come out, Lahm should be warning his fellow players and those within the sport to be more accommodating to homosexuality; after all, they may be playing in the same team as a gay player, without even realising.

While it is a fact that, at present, open homosexuality does not exist amongst mainstream professional footballers, there remains a continued debate amongst players throughout the world over whether homosexuality can ever openly exist within the game. In 2010, Bayern Munich striker Mario Gomez, like Joey Barton, expressed a belief that it could and should exist openly. He added that any gay footballers in Germany would play "as being liberated" if they were to publicly reveal their sexuality. Referring to Guido Westerwelle and Klaus Wowereit, Gomez stated: "We've got a gay vice chancellor and a gay mayor of Berlin. Footballers should own up to their preference as well." His logic is sound. If homosexuality can exist within something as unforgiving as the political arena, it should be able to exist in football as well. It also seems clear that a homosexual footballer who came out publicly would receive public backing from players like Joey Barton and Mario Gomez, and that support could be vital in helping a gay footballer to withstand any negative reaction to his decision.

However, Philipp Lahm, Gomez's Bayern Munich team mate, provided a swift rebuttal to his claims that if homosexuality can exist in the world of politics it can also exist in the world of professional football. "Westervelle doesn't have to play in front of a crowd of 60,000 people every weekend," he said. "A player who chooses to out himself has to carry out his job in front of tens of thousands of spectators."

Lahm's viewpoint was supported by Italian striker Antonio Di Natale. In 2012, after Italy coach Cesare Prandelli wrote the foreword for a book, in which he called for homosexual players to let themselves be known, Di Natale responded by arguing against his own coach's words. "I really respect Prandelli and I care about him as a person, but I don't agree with him," Di Natale said. "Breaking the taboo on homosexuality in the world of football is a difficult, if not impossible, task. How would the fans react? We cannot predict everyone's reaction."

This raises another major issue which confronts homosexual footballers when considering the choice of whether to open up about their sexuality: the fear of how supporters would react to the presence of an openly homosexual footballer in the twenty-first century.

Chapter Four:
Silenced by Supporters?

There is sufficient evidence to support the viewpoint that football is an institutionally homophobic sport, because of the attitudes and behaviour of those who make a living from the game. However, it is also fair to say that external factors have played a part in creating the current culture of silence that surrounds the topic of homosexuality. Perhaps chief amongst these external factors is the role that football supporters have played in keeping gay footballers in the closet.

Over the years, there have been many incidents of homophobic chanting from supporters, aimed at both players and opposing fans, and these incidents have created the distinct impression that an openly gay footballer would be subjected to extreme levels of abuse from spectators. For a homosexual footballer at the top level of the game, who regularly plays in front of tens of thousands of supporters every weekend, the attitude of those supporters is obviously going to be a major consideration before they make the decision to go public with their sexual orientation. It is unlikely that any player will willingly subject himself to abuse, especially when it can be avoided by remaining discreet about his sexuality.

It would be wrong to imply that all football supporters are homophobic, or that they would all subject an openly gay player to abuse. On the contrary, it goes without saying that football supporters are diverse and do not all share the same views. In addition, research conducted by Staffordshire University has suggested that the majority of football supporters in the United Kingdom adopt liberal attitudes towards homosexuality, and would be happy to support a homosexual player from their own team, if he decided to open up about his sexual preference. In addition, a whopping 90% of the football supporters who took part in the study claimed they would not hold any specific hostility towards a gay player from an opposing team either. Research from Stonewall indicates that just one in six supporters believe their club is doing enough to tackle anti-gay abuse in the sport, which seems to demonstrate that supporters disagree with their club's lack of action and want to see bigger steps taken.

There have also been clear examples of supporters demonstrating tolerance for homosexuality in the sport. Fans in Sweden's lower leagues have generally behaved very well despite the presence of Anton Hysén, Europe's only openly gay footballer. Hysén's story will be covered in more depth later on in this book and, although Sweden's lower leagues are clearly not reflective of the culture that exists in Europe's top football leagues, the treatment Hysén has received from fans creates a sense of hope that the same tolerance could be established in a high-profile European league in the future.

Of course, there are also many football supporters who are gay, and so are extremely unlikely to participate in any sort of abuse towards a homosexual footballer. The establishment of the Gay Football Supporters Network has led to an increasingly visible homosexual presence amongst football fans and the network's work in encouraging gay amateur footballers to play the game has been one of the more progressive movements towards creating tolerance of homosexuality, at least at the grass roots level of the sport. In addition, in 2009, FC Barcelona became the first Spanish club to openly accept a gay and lesbian supporters group. These facts show that it is not completely impossible for homosexuality and professional football to co-exist.

Furthermore, in recent years, many heterosexual supporters have began to adopt a more relaxed attitudes towards homosexuality. This has been demonstrated by a fairly recent trend, whereby many fans have expressed their attraction to star footballers. Notable objects of this particular type of affection include Thierry Henry and David Beckham, with hundreds of supporters taking to social networking websites to insist that they would 'go gay' for the two iconic players. As Paul Flynn, a reporter for The Guardian newspaper, pointed out, the out-pouring of love from Arsenal supporters for Thierry Henry, during his brief return to the club in 2012, was reminiscent of the type of 'go-gay-for' fan worship which has long been associated with musicians like John Lennon and Morrissey. Music has, historically, been much more open to homosexuality and the similarity offers hope that football can make significant steps in the same direction. Although much of this trend can be considered tongue-in-cheek, it shows, at the very least, that there is the potential for homosexual views and opinions to be supported by heterosexual football fans.

However, the fact remains that many football supporters still hold on to homophobic views or have actually engaged in homophobic acts. While there appears to be a general feeling that, for the most part, a gay footballer would be supported by his own team's fans, the behaviour of opposition supporters is far less assured.

Despite Staffordshire University's research suggesting that the majority of football fans would not engage in homophobic abuse towards opposition players if they came out as gay, a survey conducted by Stonewall found that 70% of football fans had heard anti-gay abuse in football stadiums between the years 2004-2009. The vast majority of this abuse was aimed at opposition players. Fewer than half of the people asked felt that there was less homophobic abuse on the terraces in 2009 than there was in 1989. This research appears to indicate a worrying lack of progress in the battle against homophobia on the terraces within that twenty year period.

Examples of homophobic abuse are not difficult to find either. Former England international Sol Campbell is just one player who has been on the receiving end of homophobic abuse from rival supporters in recent years. Campbell made a controversial move from Tottenham Hotspur to their north London rivals Arsenal in the summer of 2001. Like his former Arsenal team mate, Freddie Ljungberg, Campbell has long been subject to speculation about his sexual orientation, despite the fact that he has always been involved in heterosexual relationships. Campbell even married a female interior designer, Fiona Barratt, in 2010. Tottenham fans, who had been unable to forgive Campbell's perceived betrayal of their side, used the speculation over Campbell's sexuality to attack their former hero during a match in September 2008. Supporters aimed several chants at Campbell, containing both racist and homophobic content. Amongst the words in one chant were references to homosexuality, HIV and lynching.

Although police investigating the abuse claimed in their reports that the chanting came from a significant number of the 2,500 Spurs fans in attendance, only eleven of them were charged. Four pleaded guilty to the offence and were given a three-year football banning order, as well as a fine. Another man and his 13-year-old son were also found guilty of abusing Campbell in January 2009. Court evidence revealed they had shouted taunts at him and called him, amongst other insults, a "gay boy". A further five supporters were given police cautions for aiming abuse at Campbell.

Despite being heterosexual, the abuse had a negative effect on Campbell. "I felt absolutely disgusted," Campbell told the court in a written statement. "I didn't react because of my profile and I feared I might make the situation worse and cause problems. I felt totally victimised and helpless. It has had an effect on me personally and I do not want it to continue. I support the police in their action."

Although the abuse suffered by Campbell was obviously traumatic for the player, ultimately the abuse consisted of baseless taunts. A genuinely homosexual player, however, would potentially have to deal with similar abuse, despite it hitting much closer to home. In addition, the abuse suffered by Campbell is actually a rare example of a case where homophobic abuse from supporters at a football ground was appropriately punished by the authorities. Unfortunately, more often than not, such homophobic chanting is simply allowed to slide, despite the fact that most racist abuse and other forms of discrimination would not be tolerated in the same way.

For example, Brighton & Hove Albion supporters are regularly subjected to homophobic chanting from opposing supporters. Brighton has a reputation for being the 'gay capital' of Britain, primarily due to its substantial LGBT community and large number of gay night clubs. According to the Office of National Statistics, it is the UK city with the highest proportion of same-sex couples per 1,000 residents. During the BBC Three documentary 'Britain's Gay Footballers', Amal Fashanu went to watch a Brighton & Hove Albion game and interviewed several Brighton supporters about the homophobic chanting. Within ten minutes of being at the match, Fashanu had heard such chants, which included "We can see you holding hands," "Does your boyfriend know you're here?" and "Stand up, if you can't sit down." According to the Brighton fans she interviewed, such chants take place at virtually every match. Upon leaving the match, twenty years on from the horrific abuse that her uncle received from supporters, Fashanu remarked that, even today, she found it difficult to believe that a gay footballer could be open about his sexuality. If they did decide to do so, she concluded, abuse from sections of the crowd would be an inevitability.

Similarly, music legend Elton John experienced homophobic discrimination from rival fans during his time as chairman and director of Watford Football Club. A popular chant from the time, sang by supporters to the tune of 'My Old Man (Said Follow The Van)', contained the words, "Don't sit down while Elton is around, or you might get a penis up your arse." On one occasion, when he made a trip to Blackpool's Bloomfield Road ground for an away match, Elton John was met by the chant: "He's bald, he's queer, he takes it up the rear, Elton John. Elton John." Although Elton John took the abuse in good humour and was known to laugh at some of the chants, the fact remains that not all gay men in the sport would be so comfortable with them. It is certainly problematic that the abusive chants were allowed to exist without challenge, regardless of the the fact that Elton John was able to put up with them. Again, no matter how witty or amusing it was to the victim, racial chanting towards a club chairman would not be allowed to slide.

Some of the most disturbing homophobic chants came from Ipswich Town supporters, in the aftermath of Justin Fashanu's death. Indeed, to this day, some Ipswich supporters can be heard singing the horrifying chant, "He's gay, he's dead, he's hanging in a shed, Fashanu. Fashanu." Such chanting quite clearly crosses the line of what can be considered an acceptable topic for 'banter'. It is in poor taste, is offensive to Fashanu's family and friends and acts to further discourage gay players from coming out.

Peter Clayton has expressed a belief that football supporters in England would verbally slaughter a current gay player in much the same way they did with Fashanu, if he were to open up about his sexuality. "It would take a very courageous Premier League footballer to come out because fans are so vociferous in football in a way they aren't in any other sport," he explained. It is certainly true that football supporters can be very abusive towards opposition players, preying on all kinds of personal issues. Given the homophobic abuse received by certain heterosexual footballers, especially those whose sexuality has come under question, it is probably fair to say that a gay footballer would be subjected to abuse from rival fans if he came out publicly, at least in the immediate aftermath of such a revelation.

Although England clearly has a problem with homophobic chanting from football supporters, it is perhaps even more common and, sadly, even more widely accepted in certain countries in mainland Europe.

In Germany, and other German-speaking countries, it is popular to sing "Ihr seid alle homosexuell" to the tune of the Beatles' song 'Yellow Submarine'. This chant translates to "You are all homosexuals." In 2008, when England played Spain in Seville, David Beckham was subjected to a chant of "Beckham maricón," which translates to a chant calling Beckham a "faggot". Interestingly, the match in question also contained audible racial abuse towards England players. Yet, amidst hysteria over racial abuse during the match, the homophobic abuse Beckham received was barely noted. The English FA claimed they did not even notice the abuse had taken place, once again highlighting the double standard between football's battle with racism and football's inability to effectively tackle homophobia.

In truth, the "maricón" chant is common in almost all Spanish football grounds. Former Real Madrid player, Guti, experienced it on a regular basis. What is especially interesting about homophobic abuse in Spanish football is the way that it is so clearly at odds with the rest of Spanish culture. A Eurobarometer survey, published in 2006, showed that 66% of Spanish people supported same-sex marriage, 22% more than the EU-wide average. Gay men can serve openly in the Spanish military, same-sex marriage was legalised in 2005 and gay couples were also granted adoption rights in the same year. In short, Spain adopts one of the most liberal attitudes towards homosexuality of any major nation in the world. Yet somehow, even in a country with some of the most progressive LGBT rights legislation around, homophobia in football is still a major problem.

While it would be grossly unfair to suggest all football supporters are homophobic, there is clearly enough of a homophobic presence in stadiums throughout Europe to impact upon a gay footballer's decision on whether or not to express their sexuality publicly. The use of homophobic slurs in popular chants is obviously going to discourage the presence of open homosexuality in the sport. When gay rights group Stonewall asked people why they believed there were no openly gay players in the Premier League, the most common explanation given was that supporters would direct homophobic abuse at them.

Perhaps most troubling of all is the general lack of repercussions that these supporters face. Football supporters often adopt a pack mentality and push the boundaries with their sense of humour. However, generally, it is possible to educate supporters on what is and is not acceptable. Great steps have been made in educating supporters across the world on the issue of racism. Education leads to progression. Unfortunately, it is difficult to educate fans when authorities turn a blind eye to the very existence of homophobic feeling within the sport and when football managers openly admit they would not want a gay player in their team. There is, unquestionably, an anti-gay culture within football and it makes it very difficult to discourage fans from expressing similar views.

Chapter Five:
Homosexuality in Other Sports

Football is played by over 250 million players in over 200 countries, officially making it the most popular sport on the planet. With a documented history dating back to medieval times in England, and with potential origins as far back as the third century B.C. in China, it is also surely fair to consider football the world's most culturally significant sport. By now, it has already been firmly established that homophobic feeling is prevalent within the sport, at various levels, from the authority figures at the very top of the game, right the way down to footballers themselves and even football supporters.

One of the most remarkable things about football's apparent inability to cope with homosexuality and adequately confront homophobic attitudes in the twenty-first century is the fact that other, significantly less popular sports have managed to tackle these same issues in a far more progressive way, much earlier, despite being under less obvious cultural pressure to do so. Although homosexuality is still somewhat under-represented in most professional sports, many of them have at least dealt with the emergence of openly gay athletes far more effectively than the way in which professional football dealt with Justin Fashanu in 1990.

Rugby has been particularly impressive in its efforts to embrace homosexuality. In 1995, just five years after Justin Fashanu's revelation caused so much trouble in football, rugby league player Ian Roberts came out as gay, declaring his sexuality in interviews with various magazines and television networks over the course of the year. In the process, he became the first rugby player, and the first high-profile Australian athlete in any sport, to do so. Roberts spoke openly and with a refreshing honesty about the subject. Subsequently, the response from within the sport was overwhelmingly positive and most were supportive of his decision. Many high-profile figures within the game openly backed Roberts and praised his bravery. In the aftermath of his first interviews, Paul Vautin, Peter Sterling and Steve Roach, the hosts of the NRL Footy Show, an Australian television programme which covers the National Rugby League, appeared in a poster campaign targeting homophobia. In doing so, they demonstrated a sense of unity within rugby league as a sport, as well as a desire to pre-empt any homophobic abuse aimed at Roberts as a result of his decision.

By contrast, in 2010, when the English Football Association attempted to produce an anti-homophobia video campaign, intending to use professional footballers to support their message, they were unable to find a single player willing to be associated with the cause. In the opinion of many journalists who covered the story, including Duncan White, a football correspondent for The Telegraph, this disappointing lack of support stemmed from little more than fear. The footballers contacted, it has been claimed, felt that if they featured in the campaign, they would be associated with homosexuality, and could potentially be thought of as gay in the process.

Although his sexuality was not publicly revealed until 1995, in reality, many of Robert's fellow rugby league players were aware that he was gay as far back as the late 1980s. Despite this, Roberts claims that his sexuality caused him very few problems in his career. "I'm still involved with Souths [rugby league] club and in the twenty years since I played with Rabbitohs I've never felt any serious sense of homophobia," he said in an interview with magazine The Australian. Roberts also dismissed the often-mentioned idea that a homosexual athlete's presence could potentially lead to uncomfortable changing room situations. "It was well known in rugby league circles I was gay, long before I came out. The whole locker room thing wasn't a problem, and nobody behaved any differently to me than any other player. Every gay sportsman should get up and say something if this kind of stupidity is raised again. It's offensive."

Of course, Roberts is right. The suggestion that gay men cannot be trusted to behave appropriately in a sports locker room is offensive, born of ignorance, and has no basis in reality. Yet, amazingly, it remains one of the go-to excuses for footballers and managers, when trying to excuse their sport's inability to cope with homosexuality.

Later in the same interview, Roberts suggested that more homosexual sports stars coming out to the public would work towards putting an end to the sporting world's difficult relationship with homosexuality. "When something no longer shocks people, it becomes passé," he said.

Roberts' viewpoint is certainly relevant to the world of rugby league, because of the mature approach the sport has already adopted towards the topic of homosexuality. In the future, homosexual rugby league players can look to the example that Ian Roberts has set and be relatively confident that declaring their sexuality to the public will not be detrimental to their playing career. However, this viewpoint is somewhat less applicable to the subject of homosexuality within football. While it is true that if one gay footballer came out, and others followed close behind, it could eventually create an environment where it is no longer shocking, or even newsworthy, the problem lies in the current homophobic sentiment that exists within the sport. That homophobic underbelly makes coming out an extremely unappealing burden to shoulder for any one footballer. Before football can even begin to consider having enough openly homosexual players for it to be 'passé', attitudes within the game need to change first, so that football can adequately manage the presence of even one openly gay, mainstream professional footballer.

In addition to Ian Roberts revealing his sexuality, Welshman Gareth Thomas opened up about his sexuality in an interview with the Daily Mail newspaper in December 2009, making him the first gay rugby union player to do so. Thomas, as it transpired, had been struggling to come to terms with his sexuality since the age of seventeen, largely because of the perceived pressure to conform to masculine stereotypes in the sport and to fit in with the heterosexual locker room banter. When he did eventually come out, he was in his mid-30s, and had established respect within the sport for his ability. After a difficult conversation, in which he expressed his true feelings to his wife, Thomas became racked with feelings of guilt over deceiving his childhood sweetheart for so many years. Suffering emotional turmoil, Thomas later broke down in tears in the changing room after a match. Overwhelmed, he revealed his sexuality to one of his coaches, Scott Johnson, and later made the difficult decision to come out to the rest of his team mates and, eventually, the wider world.

Again, like with Roberts, Thomas' experience in the aftermath was largely positive and he received widespread backing from within rugby union circles. The sport also took steps to limit homophobic reaction from supporters. When Thomas was subjected to anti-gay abuse from Castleford fans, the Yorkshire club was promptly fined £40,000 for their actions. It represented a firm stance from those in charge of the game that not only would abuse not be tolerated, but those who engage in such behaviour would only be damaging their own team. That incident aside, Thomas has largely been treated with respect by rugby fans.

The reaction of his team mates at the Cardiff Blues was even more positive. The first two to find out were his friends, Stephen Jones and Martyn Williams. "I sat in the bar waiting for them, I was absolutely terrified, wondering what they were going to say," he told the Daily Mail. "But they came in, patted me on the back and said: 'We don't care. Why didn't you tell us before?' Two of my best mates in rugby didn't even bat an eyelid." This positivity was then replicated by the rest of his team mates and by other staff members at the club. "No one distanced themselves from me. Not one single person," Thomas explained.

When Amal Fashanu later interviewed Thomas during her BBC documentary on homosexuality in football, she asked him for his opinion on the differences between football and rugby's ability to cope with the presence of homosexuality. In response, Thomas expressed a belief that the key difference was in how those in charge of the game dealt with the subject. While Thomas, like Roberts before him, received firm backing from the higher-ups in his sport, there remains little assurance that the same would happen to a gay footballer. On the contrary, it has already been confirmed that many football managers and club chairmen would look to kick a gay player out of their club. Thomas believes that the backing he received from within rugby league was crucial in ensuring that his sexuality was accepted by both supporters and players alike. Speaking specifically about football, Thomas explained to Fashanu, "I think if the FA were to come out and make a statement saying, you know, 'we will stamp on anything [homophobic] it would create a safer environment."

In 2010, Gareth Thomas was named top of the IoS 'Pink List', which ranks the 101 most influential gay and lesbian people in Britain. In the same year, he also received the 'Hero of the Year' award from Stonewall and was praised as a hero by television presenter Ellen DeGeneres. Gareth Thomas serves as a potential role model to gay athletes in any sport and clearly rugby, as a team sport with a perceived macho image, can provide a blueprint for football to follow in terms of how to deal with homosexual athletes. It essentially proves that homosexuality could exist in football as well, if the right measures were taken. All football really needs is a unified desire throughout the sport to follow in the same path.

However, rugby is not the only sport that can teach football lessons on how to effectively deal with subject of homosexuality. English cricketer Steven Davies gave an interview with The Daily Telegraph in February 2011, in which he also came out as gay, making him the first international cricketer to do so. In the interview, Davies spoke of how Gareth Thomas had served as an inspiration for him in making his own decision to go public. Like with Thomas, Davies found that coming out provided him with a sense of closure. "I'm comfortable with who I am – and happy to say who I am in public," he told the Telegraph. "To speak out is a massive relief for me."

Once again, as with Thomas and Roberts before him, Davies received total backing from many of those within his sport. England team director Andy Flower released a public statement confirming that Davies' decision to speak openly about his sexuality would not impact upon his international career. "I would like to make it very clear that Steve is first and foremost a very talented cricketer and a valued member of the England set-up," he said. "His private life is his own concern and has absolutely no bearing on his ability to excel at the very highest level in international sport...Steve has had and will continue to have the full respect and support of the entire squad and everyone involved in England cricket."

Vikram Solanski, the chairman of the Professional Cricketer's Association, also firmly defended Davies' decision. "Steve has the full support of all his colleagues in cricket. Many of those he plays with and against have known about this for some time, and none of them regard it as anything other than an entirely personal matter." he explained. Both statements sent a clear message that the player's sexuality was not going to hinder his career as a cricketer.

Ian Bell, a team mate of Davies, offered his own support, while stating that, in his opinion, homosexuality is not a taboo subject in cricket in the same way that it is in football. "I can't speak for other teams and other sports," he said. "But for us as a group, it didn't affect anything for Steve or any of the other lads. It helped him by speaking to the guys and we just got on with it. He's a fantastic cricketer and we are all with him."

Once again, a crucial element in cricket's success at dealing with homosexuality was the backing that Davies received from people in charge, who, in the process, set a clear example to players and fans on how to deal with the matter. Given the prevailing attitudes of authority figures in football and some of the immature attitudes that have been displayed by professional footballers, it is difficult to see football offering a gay player the same opportunity to succeed. Certainly, Justin Fashanu was not afforded the luxury of widespread backing and understanding in the 1990s and was instead condemned by many of his colleagues. There has been little evidence of progress since.

Within certain circles, there exists a belief that homosexuality is a more complicated issue within team sports than it is within solo sports. Given that, it is worth assessing the validity of the viewpoint. Matthew Mitcham made headlines for being one of the few openly gay athletes competing in the 2008 Olympic Games in Beijing. Mitcham represented Australia and won a gold medal in the men's 10-metre platform diving event. Despite his success, Mitcham found it difficult to attract sponsorship deals and has openly expressed a suspicion that his sexuality has played a part in that. This suggests that homosexual athletes in solo sports also face difficulties in their career. However, the crucial point is that they are still able to be open and honest about their sexuality, without facing widespread abuse. Mitcham has expressed that, despite his difficulties, he has absolutely no regrets about expressing his sexuality openly. In the aftermath of Mitcham's success in Beijing, he received many letters of support from gay teenage fans; a fact which helped to confirm that he had made the right choice. "That was really nice, really humbling," he told journalist Steve Dow.

These examples of homosexual sports stars succeeding in other sports should offer a hope that, one day, a gay footballer can enjoy similar success. Perhaps, in the future, football will be able to learn lessons from these other sports on how to deal with the issue. The presence of gay athletes in other sports can also teach football a lesson about exactly why it is so important for homosexual footballers to have the opportunity to express their sexuality openly if they wish.

Gareth Thomas has admitted that he personally struggled to come to terms with his sexuality, partially because of the pressure he felt he was under to adhere to the stereotypes associated with his sport. More worryingly, he also admitted that he had contemplated suicide before he eventually reached the point where he felt comfortable enough with his sexuality to let it be known to the public. This highlights a fairly common problem for people in the LGBT community. For a homosexual person, coming to terms with their sexuality can be an extremely difficult and complicated process. Often they feel that making their sexuality known, whether to family members, friends or strangers, can act as a huge relief and offer closure to internal struggles, enabling them to fully accept themselves for who they are. Sports which openly advise their gay athletes to remain closeted, like football has done, instead simply offer gay athletes yet another obstacle to overcome. Gareth Thomas felt a sense of relief in revealing his sexuality to the world, especially when he realised that the reaction to his sexuality was not nearly as negative as he expected. It subsequently made the quality of his personal life better. By creating a 'don't ask, don't tell' culture, football effectively denies any gay players this possibility. Those who think homophobia is anything other than a major issue in football should consider the fact that a gay footballer, right now, could be suffering the same suicidal thoughts as Thomas experienced, with no means of alleviating the pressure.

In addition, almost every openly gay sports star speaks of the lack of gay role models in sport, and the knock-on effect that has on young homosexual men and women. In light of his own experience, Thomas is now keen to act as a potential role model to gay youngsters. "I'm proud of who I am," he said. "I feel I have achieved everything I could ever possibly have hoped to achieve out of rugby, and I did it being gay. I want to send a positive message to other gay people that they can do it, too." Thomas has also become a vocal supporter of ChildLine, a British charity which offers telephone counselling services for young people. Speaking of his own contemplation of suicide, the work the charity does and his own influence, he said: "I don't know if my life is going to be easier because I'm out, but if it helps someone else, if it makes one young lad pick up the phone to ChildLine, then it will have been worth it."

Ian Roberts has also spoken out about how important he feels it is for gay sports stars to visibly come out as being gay, while active in sport. Although a person's sexuality is in many ways a deeply personal issue, Roberts feels that the presence of visible gay role models in sport is important for young people and that gay sports stars should perhaps even feel an obligation to make their sexuality known, for the greater good. "It breaks down stereotypes like nothing else, especially for young men," Roberts explained. "There are gay kids in the suburbs and the country who are killing themselves because they see only a limited depiction of gay people that they don't fit. If you don't think this is a serious problem, look at the statistics. Gay teens are about the most likely to commit suicide."

The message is clear; it is vitally important for gay teenagers to have positive role models to look up to, especially in sport, where homosexuality has been under-represented for so long. Athletes like Thomas, Roberts and Mitcham have demonstrated a strong sense of pride at being able to provide a positive example for the current generation of youth, many of whom may be struggling to come to terms with their own sexuality.

This is part of the reason why it is so important for football, as the world's premier sport, to follow suit and treat homophobia as seriously as it treats racism and other cultural issues.

Football may be the world's leading sport in terms of the number of spectators it has, yet it remains embarrassingly behind other sports in dealing with what should by now be a fairly straightforward issue. Denying the presence of homosexuality in football and expecting homosexual athletes to keep quiet not only hurts the athletes themselves, but it also hinders future generations of youngsters.

Chapter Six:
The Role of the Media

Media coverage of sport in the twenty-first century is a huge industry, and football is at the forefront of that industry throughout most of Europe and, indeed, much of the rest of the world. Now, perhaps more than at any other time in history, football dominates large sections of the media. In countries like Spain and Italy, there are multiple newspapers dedicated entirely to the sport. In the United Kingdom there have been several 24-hour sports news channels, which focus almost entirely on football. Television coverage of the sport is at its highest ever level, and every season it seems more live matches and highlights are shown on television. The invention and expansion of the internet has only added to the interest that football generates across the globe.

Clearly, such huge media interest in the sport is, in many ways, hugely beneficial to the game, its teams and its players; especially from a financial perspective. Unfortunately, however, when it comes to the subject of homosexuality in football, the media also plays a large role in both creating and sustaining widespread acceptance of anti-gay sentiment, especially amongst supporters.

One way in which the media plays a role in creating homophobic feeling within the sport is by constantly reinforcing overly masculine stereotypes and, perhaps more importantly, by using homophobic slurs to describe footballers who are not perceived to be living up to those stereotypes. An example of this was found in the English media in the aftermath of the 2006 FIFA World Cup, with the way certain newspapers described Portugal's star player, Cristiano Ronaldo. The Sun used terms like "Portuguese nancy boy" to describe the winger, while other newspapers chose to mock his supposedly gay dress sense. Peter Tatchell, through gay rights group Outrage, released a statement condemning The Sun, in particular, for their reporting. Tatchell also urged the Football Association to take legal action against the newspaper.

"The Sun's homophobic sneers against Portuguese football star, Cristiano Ronaldo, are out of order," Tatchell said in the statement. "We urge the Football Association to prove its proclaimed commitment to tackling homophobia by reporting The Sun to the Press Complaints Council. The Sun branded Ronaldo a 'nancy boy' [and] stirred up homophobic prejudice against Ronaldo, with its sneering insinuation that he is gay. The Football Association has pledged to stamp out homophobia and to protect players who are victims of homophobic prejudice. It is time the FA made good its promise..."

In response, a spokeswoman for the Football Association confirmed their lack of retaliatory action. In a statement, she claimed that the FA were only concerned with footballing issues, and would not involve themselves in media debates.

Although Cristiano Ronaldo has been involved in a number of heterosexual relationships, and has not personally responded to the reports, at least publicly, with any anger, the fact remains that media organisations insulting footballers with homophobic slurs causes obvious damage to the fight for gay rights within the sport. In doing so, they also create an ideal of rugged, straight, macho footballers, while presenting perceived homosexual attributes as being negative qualities in a player. It only serves to compound fears that a gay footballer would be mocked and ridiculed by the press, something which, in this day and age, should be completely unacceptable.

The reinforcement of such stereotypically masculine ideals within football also has knock-on effects. For one, sponsors buy into the public image that the media help to mould. As a result, when a company decides to enter into a sponsorship deal with a footballer, they expect that player to live up to the same image. It has, therefore, been suggested by several people, including Professor Ellis Cashore, who led a study on the subject, that gay footballers are advised to remain in the closet in order to avoid losing sponsorship deals. In the research on homosexuality in football conducted by Staffordshire University, 40% of people asked felt agents were responsible for the lack of gay footballers, due to the fact that they advise their clients that being openly gay would hurt their commercial potential. There have been suggestions that professional football clubs are also complicit in this, feeling that having a gay footballer in their team would hurt their overall brand and global marketability, especially in countries and regions where homosexuality is still not widely accepted.

As mentioned earlier in the book, openly gay referee, John Blankenstein, was replaced as the head official for the 1994 UEFA Champions League Final, at least partially because of his sexual orientation. In that incident, the Gazzetta dello Sport, a famous sports newspaper in Italy with wide circulation, decided to point out his sexuality, amidst the existing anger at his appointment due to his nationality. In doing so, they brought the negative feeling aimed at him to new heights. The fact that his sexuality was mentioned in the newspaper is not what makes it problematic. Instead, it is the way in which it was seized upon, as part of a negative story, in order to drum up further outrage. By engaging in such insensitive reporting and making his sexuality a national focus, the newspaper helped to generate enough anger against Blankenstein that his physical well-being was threatened by Milan supporters.

Another way in which the media plays a large role in keeping gay footballers silent is through the reporting of alleged homosexual scandals. In 2006, for instance, the News of the World and The Sun both featured a story, which alleged that they had seen photographic evidence of two well-known footballers being involved in a gay orgy with a high-profile figure from the music industry. The News of the World published photographs of two men, with their identities concealed, and described the sex acts as 'perverted'. Despite being engaged to singer Cheryl Cole at the time of the allegations, and despite the fact that the newspaper did not specifically name him, England international Ashley Cole took legal action against the two papers. He felt that the photographs had been published and arranged in a way which would cause people to speculate that he was one of the footballers involved.

After beginning legal proceedings, his lawyer released a statement, which said: "These newspapers published false and offensive articles designed to tell readers that Ashley had behaved in what the News of the World described as a 'perverted' way with other professional footballers. The newspapers knew there was no basis to name Ashley but arranged the articles and pictures in such a way that readers would identify him. Ashley Cole will not tolerate this kind of cowardly journalism or let it go unchallenged."

This particular report was hugely damaging for several reasons. First of all, the nature of the report, as if the orgy was some kind of secret and sordid underground act, creates an unfavourable and offensive image of homosexuality and what it entails. Secondly, the use of the world 'perverted' to describe the alleged acts holds connotations that homosexuality is somehow abnormal and even sinister. Additionally, the inaccurate reports led to speculation on the internet about the identities of the players, creating a kind of modern day witch hunt, aimed at identifying homosexual footballers.

Most troublesome, however, has been the aftermath. Ashley Cole is still, on occasion, subjected to offensive homophobic jibes from crowds, especially from the supporters at his former club, Arsenal. The whole incident goes some way to demonstrating exactly why there are no openly gay players in England. The press attention, the attempts to scandalise alleged homosexual encounters and the homophobic abuse from supporters make it a completely unappealing prospect.

While conducting research, Stonewall spoke to several supporters who admitted that they believed anti-gay abuse in football had increased over the last twenty years. One of the explanations given for the increase was the tabloid intrusion into the lives of professional players and subsequent speculation and innuendo.

It is obvious that the media can be hugely beneficial to football as a whole, but it can also be hugely damaging, helping to form negative popular opinions amongst supporters and players alike and generally reaffirming harmful stereotypes, which limit the potential for homosexuality to become widely accepted within the sport. In many ways, the football media, filled with ex-players and managers, is also a victim of football's lack of tolerance for homosexuality in general, as many of the views expressed through the media initially stem from football changing rooms.

If attitudes within football towards homosexuality are ever going to really change, the media needs to play an active role in that change. Newspapers need to take some responsibility and report in a more ethical way; a way which is not insulting to any gay players out there and a way that does not treat homosexuality as a scandal or perversion. If a gay player in a major football nation, like England, Spain or Italy, is ever going to come out openly, it seems that sections of the media need to, at the very least, demonstrate that they will not victimise that player and, ideally, will actually support them for making such a courageous decision.

Chapter Seven:
A Glimmer of Hope

Although there are currently no openly gay, male professional football players in any of the top leagues in the world, one active European player, far away from the mainstream attention given to the top leagues of England, Spain, Italy and Germany, has taken the brave decision to come out publicly and admit to being gay. Aided in no small part by the small crowds he plays in front of in the fourth tier of the Swedish football league system, his country's liberal attitude towards homosexuality and the relative lack of media coverage he attracts, Anton Hysén, nevertheless provides gay footballers with a small sense of hope that perhaps, one day soon, the top leagues will also be able to accept the presence of openly gay professional footballers.

Growing up as the son of a successful professional footballer, Anton Hysén probably felt under a certain amount of pressure to live up to the masculine stereotype associated with them. Glenn Hysén, Anton's father, played for Liverpool in the late 1980s and early 1990s. While at the Merseyside club, Glenn firmly established himself as a tough defender and was a vital part of the team which won the league title in the 1989-90 season. It was during this time at Liverpool, in December 1990, that his son Anton was born.

In his youth, Anton displayed a serious talent for football, so decided to follow in his father's footsteps and try to make a career for himself in the sport. Although he identifies himself as being Swedish, Anton Hysén still maintains a strong connection to England and, more specifically, Liverpool, the place of his birth. He has a St. George's flag stitched onto his personalised football boots, he still openly supports Liverpool Football Club and has a reference to the club's famous motto, 'You'll Never Walk Alone', tattooed on his arm. The tattoo's message is now, perhaps, somewhat ironic, given the fact that Hysén is, at least presently, the only active gay professional player in Europe to be out of the closet; however, it remains a reassuring slogan for him.

In 2007, Hysén was offered a trainee contract by Swedish side BK Häcken and he stayed at the club until 2009. However, injuries hindered his progress at the club. At the age of 18, Hysén had a trial with Doncaster Rovers in England but was unsuccessful in winning a move to the club. Later in 2009 he signed for Utsiktens BK in Sweden. At the time of writing, he remains at the club, although he still harbours ambitions to, one day, make the journey across the North Sea to play for a top team in England.

It has often been suggested that for a gay footballer to be fully accepted, he would likely need to be an experienced player, perhaps close to retirement, who had already made his legacy in the game and earned respect for his talents. Anton Hysén does not fit this description at all. He made his decision to come out publicly at the age of just 20, via an interview with Swedish magazine Offside in 2011. He acknowledged that the decision did carry an element of risk attached to it. "Me coming out may have a bearing on my career. There are people who can't deal with homosexuals. A club may be interested to sign me but then the coach finds out that I am gay and doesn't want to sign me any more. That could happen, but then it is their problem. If I perform as a footballer, then I don't think it matters if I like boys or girls," Hysén explained.

His father, despite his former career within the deeply homophobic environment of professional football, and in spite of his own masculine public image, was fully supportive of his son's decision. In actual fact, in many ways, Glenn Hysén inspired his son to tell his story to his team mates and the world.

In 2007, at a Pride march in Stockholm, Glenn made a controversial appearance as a public speaker. The initial outrage surrounding his appearance stemmed from a previous incident in his life, back in 2001, where Glenn Hysén physically assaulted a gay man who had groped him in a public toilet. Despite the inappropriate nature of the man's advances, the incident and subsequent media fall out led to many accusing Glenn Hysén of being a typical homophobic footballer. Six years later, many people within the LGBT community were outraged by the prospect of the same man addressing them at a Pride event.

Despite these concerns, and to the surprise of many, Glenn Hysén spoke with great sincerity and empathy of a young, closeted 16-year-old professional footballer, who did not want to come out "because he feared what his team mates would think." At the time, those in attendance were impressed by the nature of his speech. They were, however, completely unaware that the 16-year-old boy he was referring to was his own son, Anton. Privately, his mother was similarly supportive of her son and in 2011, Glenn Hysén spoke to a journalist about his son's sexuality. From there, Offside decided to pursue the story and, with the backing of his family, the decision was eventually made to go public with the information.

Such firm support from within his family certainly made Anton's decision to address his sexual orientation a whole lot easier. He believes it is one of the factors which separates his story from that of Justin Fashanu over twenty years earlier. In addition, while Fashanu had to deal with Brian Clough's archaic views, Anton Hysén had the full support of the coaching staff at Utsiktens. Admittedly, it helped that his father was one of his coaches at the club, however, the support extended beyond that. His other main coach spoke to Hysén about the bravery of his decision to come out, and vowed that anyone at the club who had a problem with Hysén's sexuality would be kicked out. The move demonstrated a clear and admirable lack of tolerance for homophobia at the club. In truth, Hysén's coach had little to worry about. His team mates were almost universally supportive of his decision, and Hysén claims that he has never experienced any sort of homophobic bullying from within the club.

The general attitude towards homosexuality within Swedish society has also played an almost indisputable role in ensuring Hysén's story has a happier ending than Fashanu's. "People here are a little more liberal," he admits. Such liberal views have an obvious effect on the nature of Swedish football supporters and their reaction to his sexuality. Despite the constant fears to the contrary, generally speaking, supporters have treated Hysén with respect and even admiration. The relative lack of spectators compared to, for example, an English Premier League match, has obviously contributed towards keeping abuse to a minimum, yet it is not the only reason for his success story. In fact, many opposition fans have spoken openly of their respect for Hysén's bravery. His own team's supporters have also grown to appreciate the fact that his status as Europe's only openly gay player has increased the media exposure the club receives, both domestically and overseas, which can only be good for the club's future.

Hysén's revelation has also enabled him to establish himself as both a homosexual and general footballing role model. Indeed, his status within the game is far higher than other footballers playing in Sweden's lower tiers. Being a role model is a status that Hysén accepts, but still remains surprised by. "I was on the train last weekend and this girl said: 'you've made the world a better place, thank you for being there for everyone,'" he told Patrick Barkham in an interview with The Guardian in March 2011. "And I haven't done anything. But when you think about it, you kinda have. Obviously I haven't been playing in the top league but I'm still going for it, and I'm still the only active player who has come out, so of course it's huge." Hysén's bravery serves to make him a role model to heterosexual and homosexual supporters alike. He is also happy to serve as a role model to other gay footballers, and has personally advised them to speak to him if they would like advice or support.

However, despite the reaction to his sexuality, Hysén does not deny the existence of a problem with homophobia in football. He accepts that his own situation is drastically different from a footballer in one of Europe's top leagues, even though his own ambition is to play at such a high level. Hysén also finds the lack of a homosexual presence in top level football to be troubling. "It's completely strange, isn't it? It's all fucked up. Where the hell are all the others? No one is coming out," he told Offside.

Moreover, since coming out, Hysén's story has not been universally positive. Despite Sweden's reputation as a bastion for liberal attitudes, certain groups of opposition supporters have occasionally engaged in the homophobic jibes. In a match with Assyriska in 2011, for example, Hysén received fairly widespread abuse, including being called a "fucking faggot." Although his own performance in the match was not too badly affected by the abuse –

on the contrary it seemed to act as a motivational tool – it did little to dis-spell concerns about how football supporters in higher leagues would react to the presence of a gay player. If supporters abuse a footballer in an ultra-liberal country like Sweden, how would they react in some of Europe's more conservative countries? His mother has also been open about her own fear about the reaction he would receive from some supporters in higher leagues in Sweden. Hysén's own ability to withstand the abuse is also, frankly, besides the point. Nobody deserves to be discriminated against, at their place of work, because of their sexuality.

Thankfully, though, such abuse has been extremely rare. Overall, up until now, Hysén's story has been a largely positive tale of homosexuality prevailing in the sport, at least away from the glare of the mainstream media spotlight. Hysén's aspiration to play at a higher level, despite the homophobia that unquestionably exists there, is certainly admirable and he has had no second thoughts about his decision to come out. "I've no regrets," he told The Justin Campaign during an interview. "I personally don't see myself as a role model...but I'll do everything I can to make this world a better place."

Chapter Eight:
Back to Reality

In the aftermath of Hysén coming out to the press, many gay rights campaigners and football journalists predicted the floodgates would now open. It was initially believed that other gay footballers would start to make themselves known, because they now had a role model other than Fashanu to look up to; in this case, a gay role model in the sport, who came out publicly, and emerged with a largely positive tale to tell. However, it's easy to get carried away by the importance of Hysén's story, on a global scale. While unquestionably brave, his decision to come out was aided by many factors that do simply not apply to footballers in top leagues, or indeed to footballers who play in minor leagues in countries with a less liberal attitude than Sweden.

Throughout most of the world, gay footballers need more than a role model; they need major changes of attitudes throughout football and so, at least at the time of writing this book, Hysén's decision has not opened the floodgates for others to follow in his footsteps at all. In actual fact, only one other active gay professional player in the world has opened up about his sexuality since; a player with an even lower profile than Hysén. In addition, his experience within the game since coming out has also been significantly less positive, and could actually serve to further discourage others from travelling down the same path.

American midfielder David Testo was born in North Carolina in 1981. After an impressive high school and college football career, which included being named North Carolina state player of the year for 1998 and helping the University of North Carolina to the NCAA Championship in his junior season, he looked to turn pro. However, during his time in college, Testo had developed a reputation for being temperamental. As a result, he was, to the surprise of many, not drafted in the 2003 MLS SuperDraft, despite interest from several clubs. Instead, he signed for the Richmond Kickers in the A-League. A string of fine performances at that level, including scoring six goals and being named the 2003 A-League Rookie of the Year, led to more serious interest from MLS teams. Finally, in 2004 he signed for the Columbus Crew.

However, his playing time in Columbus was limited due to injuries and, after two seasons in which he contributed just one goal and four assists, he was released from his contract.

Following the disappointment of his time in MLS, Testo moved to the Vancouver Whitecaps, who played in USL-1, the new name for the A-League. Testo's USL-1 experience was more positive than his MLS experience and, despite missing several games due to his recurring injury problems, he was able to establish himself as a fan favourite at the club. In his first season with Vancouver he won the USL-1 Championship, scored seven goals and was named the club's Newcomer of the Year. In 2007, Testo was drafted to fellow Canadian side Montreal Impact, where he won his second USL-1 Championship.

Testo publicly announced that he was gay in November 2011, during an interview with French-Canadian station Radio Canada. He later told Outsports that his decision was motivated by similar circumstances to those which had motivated Justin Fashanu to come out in 1990. Jamie Hubbley, a 15-year-old boy from Ottawa, had taken his own life after being teased in school for being a figure skater. "I just couldn't get it out of my head," Testo admitted. "Why not step up and show these young kids it's okay to be who you are and be gay and be in sports? If I can help one person, why not? I'm not doing it for myself, I'm doing it to help others."

Testo has also stated his belief that his sexuality should not impact upon his career as a professional footballer, insisting that it should be largely irrelevant to his chosen career. "I'm homosexual, I'm gay. I did not choose [to be]. It's just part of who I am," Testo said. "And it has nothing to do with the talent of a soccer player. You can be both an excellent soccer player and gay."

While his sexuality clearly has no bearing on his ability to play football, unfortunately, within the current climate, it absolutely does impact upon his ability to make a living as a professional footballer. Despite his hopes that it would not be the case, since coming out, his sexuality has had a negative impact on his career.

Prior to coming out to the wider public, his sexuality had already been known by some of the staff and players at his club, Montreal Impact. Yet, prior to the team's entry into Major League Soccer (MLS) in the United States, and a month prior to his interview with Radio Canada, Testo was released from his contract. Testo is unsure as to whether his sexuality was the cause for his contract being terminated, although he has suggested that it was at least a significant factor in the decision-making process. It is easy to speculate on why that might be the case. It may well be that Montreal Impact felt his sexuality could impact upon their marketing potential in the new league, or that the high-profile nature of the league would be ill-suited to a homosexual footballer. Given the timing of the contract termination, a month before he came out to the general public, it is also worth considering the possibility that the club got wind of his plans to make his sexuality public and decided to distance themselves from him in advance, perhaps anticipating a media storm would follow. Having said that, this is merely speculation and, while Testo believes his sexuality played a part, it is certainly possible that the decision was made purely on the basis of his ability as a footballer. After all, Montreal Impact were about to enter into a league where the standard of opposition is much higher than what they had been playing against during Testo's time at the club and Testo had, by this point, also had a long history of injury problems in football. Montreal Impact, for their part, insist that they knew Testo was gay before they signed him in 2007 and his sexuality was not the reason for his release.

The impact his sexuality has had on his career since being released is more concrete. At the time of this book being published, Testo, despite being a fully fit 30-year-old with previous experience in MLS, is still without a club. Unlike with his release from Montreal Impact, he is *certain* his sexuality has played a role in his struggle to land a playing contract with another professional team. "I know for a fact that before I came out publicly I did have quite a bit of interest going," Testo explained during an interview with Sky Sports News' Special Report programme. "After I came out publicly, a lot of those went quiet."

The suggestion that clubs would withdraw their interest in Testo's services as a footballer, purely because they found out about his sexuality, or found out that he had gone public with his sexuality, is troubling. Sadly, it does not come as a major surprise, especially given the narrow-minded views of some of the key figures in the game, the macho stereotypes that surround the sport and the importance of marketing and sponsorship deals in modern football.

In the aftermath of Testo's interview with Radio Canada, he also received a lot of media interest, more than at any other point of his career, and it is possible that clubs decided they did not want to deal with the media circus which was surrounding him at that time.

During his interview with Sky Sports News, Testo also revealed that he had been on the receiving end of every gay footballer's worst fear; homophobic abuse from his fellow players. Before making his sexuality known to the public, it was somewhat of an open secret amongst many of the players in the league. Most of his team mates knew and were supportive of him. Unfortunately, opposition players were not so accommodating. "I don't want to be portrayed as a victim, however there were moments during competition where I did get verbal abuse from other players," he admitted. "I wouldn't want to repeat what they said." Testo, at that time, was playing in the USL, away from the glitz of MLS, yet his sexuality was still known to such an extent that he received homophobic taunting. Such an admission offers yet more compelling evidence that a player plying his trade in a major football league, where his profile would be higher and his sexuality even more well-known, would likely suffer similar homophobic abuse from players.

Testo has gone on record as saying that, prior to opening up about his sexuality, playing football was difficult for him, primarily from a psychological perspective. "I fought with it all my life, my whole career," Testo said. "Living the life of a professional athlete and being gay is incredibly difficult. It saps all of your energy." Despite this, he has also suggested that other gay footballers out there think twice before deciding to follow in his footsteps, at least within the current football environment, citing contracts, sponsorship deals and the high chances of having to endure abuse as the main reasons. Certain gay rights campaigners have criticised Testo for his stance, believing that discouraging gay players from coming out is detrimental to their cause. However, Testo is one of the few professional footballers who has actual first-hand experience of being openly gay within football and, clearly, his career has suffered as a result. It seems somewhat unfair to suggest he is in the wrong when, in all likelihood, he is simply looking out for the best interests of other gay players. Surely Testo cannot be blamed for the fact that football is incapable of coping with homosexuality. That said, there is an argument to suggest he should, instead, focus on encouraging others to accept homosexuality in the sport; although, in fairness, that is much easier said than done, especially for someone with such a low profile in the sport on a global scale.

Testo also claims that, since going public, he has spoken to a "surprising" amount of gay footballers who have not yet made their sexuality known to the public. Given his experience in the sport, and his struggle to find a team since coming out, it may be for the best that they have chosen to remain closeted, at least for now. However, this simply highlights the need for changes in the sport. The fact that a gay player has openly advised others not to follow in his footsteps, through fear of discrimination, is nothing short of absurd and the fact that he may be justified in doing so is a truly sad indictment of football's inability to join the modern world and accept homosexuality.

Chapter Nine:
Homophobia In Women's Football

Although this book is primarily concerned with homophobia within the men's game, it is interesting to briefly look at the attitude towards homosexuality in women's football as well. Despite being caught up in his own homophobic scandals, and despite the prevalence of homophobic attitudes within football, Sepp Blatter has used women's football as an example of football's ability to cope with homosexuality. He told The Times: "Football is open for everybody. Look at women's football. Homosexuality is more popular there."

Blatter's statement is true, at least on the surface. Open homosexuality is much more common in the women's game, with several high profile players and coaches being open about their sexual orientation. In England, national team coach Hope Powell is openly homosexual and, despite engaging in heterosexual relationships during her own playing career, she has set a fairly clear example to women playing the game that homosexuality can exist within the sport.

Meanwhile, on the continent, Germany, in particular, has adopted a very supportive attitude towards homosexuality in women's football. In 2010, German international goalkeeper Nadine Angerer told newspaper Die Zeit that she was bisexual. "I am very open about this, because I am of the opinion that there are nice guys and nice women," she said. In subsequent interviews, Angerer revealed that her decision to come out was not a difficult one and that she was unable to envision any problems stemming from her coming out. Second-choice goalkeeper Ursula Holl has been similarly open about her sexuality. In 2010, Holl and her girlfriend entered into a same-sex union and she received backing from most within the international set up.

Despite this, Holl has personally recommended that male players do not follow in her footsteps. "The more you disclose about your personal life, the more vulnerable you are. And the fans in the stadium can be very, very cruel. These public hostilities would be difficult to bear...I would not advise any [male] football player to come out."

In addition, while homosexuality may be more widely accepted in women's football than it is in the men's game, discrimination based on sexuality is still fairly widespread. Many women in the game face assumptions that they are lesbians, purely because they play football and, as a result, the sport's appeal to heterosexual women has been damaged. More problematic, however, is the victimisation that lesbian women have faced in the sport. Perhaps the most troublesome stories of homophobia in women's football stem from the African continent.

Eudy Simelane was a South African footballer who played as a midfielder for the country's national women's football team. As one of the first women from Kwa Thema, her home town, to live openly as a lesbian, Simelane was a vocal LGBT activist. In April 2008, at the age of 31, she was brutally beaten, gang raped and murdered. The subsequent autopsy found that she had suffered nine stab wounds to her chest, face and legs. According to a report from ActionAid, backed by the South African Human Rights Commission, the murder was a hate-crime, committed against Simelane because of her sexual orientation. In the aftermath, Triangle, a gay rights organisation, spoke out on the trend for 'corrective rape' in South Africa, whereby men rape lesbian women in a supposed effort to 'cure' them of homosexuality.

In 2009, one man confessed to being involved in her rape and murder, implicating three other men in the process. Those men stood trial later in the year, although only one was convicted, having been unable to explain the presence of Simelane's blood on his jeans. The other two men walked free, with the judge simply telling them they may have to face God one day over their actions.

Clearly, the horrific murder of Eudy Simelane, if it was in fact motivated by her sexual orientation, is an extreme example of an incident of violence committed against an openly homosexual footballer. That said, it does also clearly demonstrate the kind of problems that can potentially manifest, even in this day and age, if homophobic attitudes are allowed to exist without challenge and spiral out of control.

In recent years, similar homophobic attitudes within the women's game have also been clearly visible in Nigeria. In 2009, just prior to being offered the job as head coach of Nigeria's women's team, Eucharia Uche remarked that she felt the presence of lesbian players in the national team squad was "worrisome." After taking the job, she referred to homosexuality as being "morally very wrong" and a "dirty issue." The Nigerian Football Federation openly backed Uche's views. The Chief Media Officer for the NFF, Ademola Alajire, explained that the players in the squad had promised to stop engaging in homosexual acts and the NFF, for their part, claimed to have put measures in place to ensure that the players stuck to their word.

Meanwhile, during James Peters' time as technical assistant for the team, reports emerged that he had personally identified lesbian players on the team and either kicked them out of the squad or banned them from sharing rooms for each other, through fear that they would engage in homosexual acts behind closed doors. Quite why he concerned himself with what they got up to behind closed doors remains unclear, however, Peters even admitted he removed some players from the national team squad "not because they were not good good players, but because they were lesbians."

Given what has already been written before in this book, it should come as no major surprise to learn that such open discrimination against homosexual players exists within a major football federation. It will also come as little surprise to learn that FIFA were widely criticised for their lack of reaction to some of these homophobic views, despite Sepp Blatter's insistence that football is an inclusive sport, open to people of all sexualities and despite him specifically using women's football as an example of football's general tolerance of homosexuality.

So to what extent can the experiences of homosexual players in women's football be considered applicable to the men's game? First, it must be accepted that there are vast differences between the two. In many European countries, homosexuality in the women's game is widely accepted and, perhaps, even expected. The lack of mainstream media attention on the sport certainly helps, in as much as the players do not have to worry about having their every move monitored by tabloid journalists. However, in some ways, it could be said that football's ultra-masculine stereotypes are still in effect in the women's game, only this time they work to stereotype female players as being masculine lesbian figures, rather than macho hard-men.

The examples of homophobia in African women's football may seem extreme and, given that they are largely fuelled by religious views in the region, they may not even be applicable to the football leagues throughout the rest of the world. However, they still demonstrate the extent to which homophobia in football exists, largely unreported by the football media. More worrying is the fact that it is allowed to exist under the FIFA umbrella, while Sepp Blatter openly tells anyone who will listen that homosexuality is accepted in the sport. This offers yet more evidence that the football authorities do not take the issue of homophobia seriously enough, or that they are ignorant to the extent of the problem.

Chapter Ten:
Promoting Homosexuality in Football

Despite an overall lack of effort from football authorities to tackle the problem of homophobia in the sport, in recent years certain other groups have made a conscious effort to try and fight back against the anti-gay feeling that exists. These efforts can hopefully go some way to creating a future where top level professional football can be considered a genuinely inclusive sport, open to talented sportsmen, regardless of their sexual orientation.

'The Justin Campaign', named after Justin Fashanu, was launched in May 2008. The campaign aims to raise awareness of homophobia in football, challenge the stereotypes and misconceptions that exist and increase LGBT involvement in the sport at non-league level. A year after the campaign's launch, the Justin Fashanu All-Stars played their first competitive match. In a unique attempt to promote tolerance and harmony in the sport, the All-Stars team is open to absolutely anyone who wishes to play for them, regardless of sexuality or gender identity. "We felt that the Campaign should raise awareness about homophobia in football by playing football," explained founding director, Jason Hall. "You can talk all day, but it's not until you seriously compete on the pitch that people will seriously think about sexuality and football."

Football v Homophobia is an international initiative, stemming from a debate held between the Justin Campaign and Kick It Out, in association with English club Brighton & Hove Albion. Established in 2009, the initiative has continued to grow and, in 2011, received backing from the FA for tackling homophobia and prejudice against the LGBT community throughout football. The size of the task ahead was made clear in 2012, when Football v Homophobia wrote to all 160 professional clubs in England, asking them to take action against homophobia in the sport. 144 of the clubs either failed to respond or refused to support the campaign. These clubs included major Premier League sides like Manchester United, Manchester City, Chelsea and Tottenham. Indeed, out of the Premier League teams asked, only Arsenal, Aston Villa, Fulham, Liverpool, Newcastle United and Norwich City initially signed up to Football v Homophobia. Nevertheless, the initiative has at least made positive steps in getting clubs involved in the fight against discrimination in football.

Stonewall also continue to challenge homophobic views within football. The group has made significant steps in pushing for equal rights in other areas, including same-sex civil partnerships and helped to overturn a ban on homosexuals entering the armed forces. Hopefully, over time, similar progress can be made in football. In 2009, Stonewall published a report on anti-gay abuse in the sport, entitled 'Leagues Behind'. The group also has its own football team, Stonewall FC, which promotes awareness of homophobia in the game.

Meanwhile, in July 2012, Liverpool Football Club announced their intention to take part in the city's Pride event, scheduled for August 2012. In doing so, they became the first Premier League club in history to announce that they will be officially represented at a LGBT Pride event. Ian Ayre, the club managing director, expressed his belief that Liverpool's appearance at the event demonstrated a real effort to tackle homophobia. "We continue to demonstrate our commitment to ensuring that equality and principles of inclusion are embedded into all areas of Liverpool Football Club and for many years, we have taken positive steps to promote our stance against homophobia both on and off the pitch," he said. "I am delighted to confirm that some club employees and members from the Liverpool Ladies squad will be participating in the event on 4 August."

The club's decision to march at Liverpool Pride was met with widespread praise from the LGBT community. As a result, Pride representatives encouraged other football teams to get involved in the event and, a few weeks later, Liverpool's local rivals, Everton, also announced their own involvement in the march, with the club's official charity, Everton in the Community, choosing to take a stall at the celebration. "Everton in the Community prides itself on pioneering programmes to tackle issues which are often taboo in football and will work hard to demonstrate our commitment to the LGBT community," explained Jackie Twort, the charity's community engagement manager. Once again, the club were commended for their decision to participate.

While, undoubtedly, the decisions made by Liverpool and Everton to support the Pride event in their city represent a progressive step and a commitment to fighting homophobia in football and, indeed, in all walks of life, the impact of the decision is somewhat diminished by one key fact; none of the first team players from either club will be involved. This lack of representation from the players can potentially be explained by factors such as pre-season tour commitments, however, it is obvious that if players had been present at the event, the impact of the two clubs' involvement would have been significantly increased. Given the refusal of top players to feature in an FA campaign against homophobia, and given the difficulty gay rights campaigners have had in even getting players to discuss the issue, it is difficult to discount the possibility that players simply refused to take part. Regardless of the real reason for the lack of player support, it must, once again, ultimately go down as a campaign against homophobia which has failed to receive backing from top professional players.

Nonetheless, it does, at the very least, reflect a desire from the two clubs to be seen to act against homophobia in football and to support LGBT rights in the wider community; something which has certainly not been the case for many other Premier League clubs over the years.

In Italy, homophobia in football became a major issue in 2012, especially in the aftermath of Alessandro Cecchi Paone's book on homosexuality in sport. Cecchi Paone wrote that there were two gay players in the Italian national team and one bisexual; claiming he knew this for a fact because he had been involved in a relationship with one of the players. In the aftermath, much of the Italian media began to support the push for open homosexuality in the sport and spoke out against homophobic abuse.

Football still has a long way to go in its battle against homophobic discrimination. The fact that 144 of the 160 professional clubs in England were, for whatever reason, unwilling to back Football v Homophobia demonstrates the full scale of the problem and, comparatively, England has a more liberal approach to homosexuality than many other countries, which suggests there is an even bigger battle to change attitudes on a global scale.

There are, however, positive signs. Especially given the fact that major clubs like Liverpool and Everton have began to visibly back the cause, even without being specifically asked or encouraged to do so. Hopefully this will encourage other clubs to follow their lead and take action against anti-gay discrimination in football.

Chapter Eleven:
Conclusions

It is a statistical probability that, right now, there are dozens of active homosexual players competing in the top football leagues around the world, yet, currently, none of them are open about their sexuality. Professional football has a problematic relationship with homosexuality and the homophobic feeling within the sport is both widespread and hugely damaging. Several high-profile figures have demonstrated ignorance and a complete inability to approach the subject with the maturity and sensitivity that it requires and some top football managers have even publicly expressed their stance that they would kick homosexual players out of their team if they became aware of their sexuality.

This book has hopefully demonstrated that homophobic feeling exists at almost all levels within the sport, including amongst supporters, players and the media. But it is the attitudes of those within FIFA, UEFA and various football associations around the world that are perhaps the most disappointing of all, especially given the depth of resources at their disposal; resources which could easily be used to tackle the problem head-on.

Homophobia within the sport perhaps gets less mainstream attention than other social issues, such as racism and sexism, because of the lack of openly homosexual players in the game. Examples of ethnic minorities and women in the sport are highly visible, so the victims of racist and sexist abuse are highly visible too. This is not the case with gay players, and the result is that homophobia is allowed to exist, in many cases, without being challenged. However, the lack of openly homosexual players is clearly linked to that same homophobia, so a catch-22 situation has developed, whereby gay players are seemingly needed to make major changes, yet top level gay players feel like they cannot be open within the current climate, unless they wish to damage their career as a footballer. A 'don't ask, don't tell' culture, similar to that associated with many nations' armed forces, has been created, and while it may serve to prevent open discrimination against any specific homosexual player, it is also detrimental to any attempts to promote equality within the game.

Some people may, rightly, think that a person's sexuality is a deeply personal issue and not the business of supporters, the media, or, indeed, anyone else for that matter. Yet, several gay athletes in other sports have spoken of their own internal struggles and the subsequent relief that being open about their sexuality has given them. Regardless of whether or not this is the case for everyone, the key point is that in this day and age, a homosexual athlete should at least have the choice of being open about their sexuality if they wish to be. Football has created a culture where this choice is made extremely difficult and perhaps even impossible for a top level gay player, who instead has to consider the effect that coming out will have on relationships with team mates, supporters and coaching staff, as well as the damage it could cause to their own personal sponsorship opportunities and marketing potential.

The first time that the full extent of homophobic feeling within the sport was truly exposed was during the career of Justin Fashanu, the world's first openly gay professional player. Fashanu experienced anti-gay discrimination throughout his playing days, including at the hands of one of the most respected managers to ever work in the game, Brian Clough. Clough's narrow-minded views on what a footballer should be had a destructive impact on Fashanu's career; a career which had promised so much and ultimately failed to live up to expectations. After his experience with Clough, Fashanu became a journeyman footballer, only occasionally displaying glimpses of the ability that made him into Britain's first £1 million black player. In the aftermath of coming out to the public via a tabloid newspaper, anti-gay feeling within football hit new heights. His brother, and fellow professional, John Fashanu publicly insulted Justin, claiming he was a footballing outcast; and that's exactly what he was. He was an outcast for daring to speak out and admit that, yes, you can be a top-level player and gay at the same time. Abuse from supporters and the media followed, he struggled to find a permanent club in the aftermath of coming out and Fashanu's personal life soon spiralled out of all control.

The rejection that Fashanu experienced ultimately played a role in his decision to take his own life. As a result of his death, Fashanu's career and life story set a damaging precedent for gay players being open about their sexuality in the sport. However, it is important to remember that Justin Fashanu had many emotional problems in his life. Having been orphaned at a young age, he grew up confused about his own identity and seemed to suffer from other, perhaps undiagnosed, mental health issues. His decision to take his own life was made amidst serious allegations about his sexual conduct. That said, football played a role in his death and football seriously failed him during his life. That should not be swept under the carpet.

Fashanu's legacy on the game, however, goes beyond putting other gay players off of coming out. Indeed, much of the progress that *has* been made on the topic of homosexuality in football is as a result of Fashanu's story. In addition, the Justin Campaign, set up in his honour, continues to promote the sport amongst homosexual players at non-league level, which, going forward, can only have a positive influence on the general attitude towards gay players in the sport.

Unfortunately, however, it remains clear that while Fashanu's career should have taught authorities many lessons, many of those lessons were not learned. Two further players, far away from the mainstream spotlight, have come out in the years since Fashanu died and both have experienced at least some degree of homophobic abuse and discrimination. In the case of David Testo, coming out publicly has demonstrably hindered his career as a professional footballer, making it incredibly difficult for him to find a club. That gives out a clear warning that a footballer with a higher profile, playing at a higher level, in front of more supporters and with more media attention on them, would likely suffer damage to their own career. Footballers continue to be warned of that fact and, so far, all of the top level gay players are taking heed of that warning. Amongst all of this, it seems to have gone unnoticed that football's acceptance of that attitude, in this day and age, is ridiculous. In what other occupation could you be so openly homophobic and face absolutely no repercussions?

On the rare occasions that governing bodies decide to act against homophobia in football, the reach of their campaigns is limited by the lack of support they are able to generate within the game. Clubs are generally, for the most part, not interested in getting involved in anti-homophobia campaigns and many top clubs have flat-out refused to even speak about the subject of anti-gay discrimination in sport. Several professional players have been approached to take part in video or poster campaigns against homophobia, and subsequently refused, while others have refused to even speak about the subject during interviews or documentaries out of a fear of being thought of as gay. This is in stark contrast to the more mature approach taken by heterosexual players in rugby, some of whom were backing anti-homophobia campaigns decades ago. Worse still, some footballers have expressed their own anti-gay feelings, which in turn works to keep gay players in the closet out of fear of alienating their own team mates. It's a sad truth that many in the sport are still stuck in the dark ages when it comes to their views on homosexuality.

It is all well and good pointing out where football goes wrong with its views on homosexuality and giving examples of homophobia in the sport, but what can ultimately be done to improve the current situation?

Well, the first step is for governing bodies and other football authorities to take the issue of homophobia much more seriously than they currently do. That means not simply releasing statements saying that they take the issue seriously, not just making baseless claims that football is accepting of people from all backgrounds and not allowing people in powerful positions to demonstrate their own homophobic views without punishment. FIFA needs to treat homophobia every bit as seriously as racism, sexism and other forms of discrimination. The authorities within professional football need to take a long, hard look at the countless other team sports which are perceived to have the same ultra-masculine image, and learn lessons from how they have coped with the presence of homosexuality. Money needs to be invested into educating everyone involved in the game, from players to coaches to supporters, so that people know that homophobia is unacceptable. And when homophobic abuse does take place, sufficient action needs to be taken against the perpetrators, to send a clear message that it will not be tolerated.

In addition, while it may be right for a PR advisor like Max Clifford to advise gay players to stay in the closet, football associations and other leading authority groups in football should really be promoting the opposite message. Clifford's advice is a direct result of football's inability to cope with homosexuality. The attitudes of football associations are at the root of the problem. In reality, football associations should be sending a clear message that if a homosexual player chooses to be open about his sexuality, they will back him in the same way that rugby and cricket authorities backed their sports stars when faced with the same situation. If they made their support more clear, gay players would give much more consideration to the idea of coming out.

Many professional players also need to take a serious look at themselves and re-evaluate their own attitudes towards homosexuality. A lot of problems could be solved if heterosexual players educated themselves on the issue and stopped being afraid to speak out in support of gay players. After all, statistically speaking, there's a pretty good chance that many of these players know a gay footballer themselves and are completely unaware of the issues they are going through. In Germany, Mario Gomez spoke up in support of gay footballers and he was not perceived to be gay as a result. Joey Barton has also spoken out on the issue without facing any major accusations of being gay. The idea that getting involved in campaigning against anti-gay abuse in the sport would lead to those types of accusations is based on very little substance.

However, these players could make a real difference if they visibly came out in support of open homosexuality in the sport and took a firm stance against homophobia.

Supporters will also have to play a role if we are to see openly gay players in the top football leagues. The problem here is that supporters sometimes need to be educated about what is and is not acceptable 'banter' on the terraces. Many supporters still clearly believe that homophobic chants are acceptable. If the authorities sent out a clear message that homophobic abuse will not be tolerated, and if the authorities subsequently acted upon any homophobic chanting that does occur, it is likely that the problem would gradually stop. Although most supporters claim that they would be supportive of a gay player in their own team, there is still a long way to go in terms of eradicating anti-gay abuse in football grounds and, once again, the onus has to be on the sport's authorities to take a firm grip of the situation and work towards putting an end to it.

Progress will also rely on the media taking on more responsibility than they currently do. Although, in recent times, there have been television documentaries and occasional newspaper articles on the subject, the fact remains that sections of the media have to shoulder some of the responsibility for making homosexuality seem like such an alien concept in football. If the push for gay rights in football had large-scale media backing, it would be almost unstoppable. However, at the moment, many sections of the media, especially tabloid newspapers, focus instead on homosexual scandals and gossip and reinforce the current stereotypes. These things only encourage gay players to shy away from the spotlight and remain closeted about their sexuality.

It is difficult to predict when football will really make a major breakthrough in its battle with homophobia. Many figures within the game today have made predictions that we will see openly gay players, playing for high-profile clubs in the top football leagues in the world at some point within the next ten years. That may seem like a reasonable prediction, but then people would likely have said the same if the suggestion had been made in the year 2000, and the subsequent decade produced no such thing. If footballing authorities start to make changes now and take firm action against anti-gay abuse and homophobia at all levels, it is certainly possible that we may see openly gay players before too long. However, even with changes made and the backing of those in charge, a huge amount damage has already been done by the homophobia that has been allowed to exist within the sport for so long. It may, therefore, still take gay players some time to fully trust in football's ability to handle homosexuality.

Hopefully, this book has gone some way towards explaining the full scale of the problem ahead. As the world's most popular sport, surely the time has come for football to embrace a significant section of society that, until now, has been unfairly excluded from the sport at the highest level.

Bibliography:

Books / Documents:

Tony Blackshaw, Tim Crabbe, *New Perspectives on Sport and 'Deviance'* (Routledge, 2004)

Brian Clough, *Cloughie: Walking on Water* (Headline Book Publishing, 2002)

Brian Clough, *Clough The Autobiography* (Partridge Press, 1994)

Paul Freeman, *Ian Roberts: Finding Out* (Random House, 1997)

Emma Healey, *Stonewall 25: The Making of the Lesbian and Gay Community in Britain* (Virago Press, 1994)

Gabriel Kuhn, *Soccer vs. The State: Tackling Football and Radical Politics* (PM Press, 2011)

Leagues Behind (Stonewall, 2009)
<http://www.stonewall.org.uk/documents/leagues_behind.pdf>

Television:

Inside Sport: The Last Taboo – BBC One (May 2010)

Britain's Gay Footballers - BBC Three (February 2012)

Football's Last Taboo: Special Report - Sky Sports News (March 2012)

Websites:

Barkham, Patrick. "Anton Hysen: 'Anyone afraid of coming out should give me a call'"
<http://www.guardian.co.uk/football/2011/mar/29/anton-hysen-afraid-coming-out> (Accessed March 2012)

Bearak, Barry. "Mixed Verdict in Trial for South African Lesbian's Death"
<http://www.nytimes.com/2009/09/23/world/africa/23safrica.html?_r=2> (Accessed May 2012)

Bignell, Paul & Chorley, Matt. "Football's new hate shame as top clubs snub drive on homophobia"
<http://www.independent.co.uk/sport/football/news-and-comment/footballs-new-hate-shame-as-top-clubs-snub-drive-on-homophobia-7181062.html> (Accessed June 2012)

Burt, Jason. "Euro 2012: Italy striker Antonio Cassano's joke over gay players backfires spectacularly"
<http://www.telegraph.co.uk/sport/football/teams/italy/9327953/Euro-2012-Italy-striker-Antonio-Cassanos-joke-over-gay-players-backfires-spectacularly.html> (Accessed June 2012)

Campbell, Denis. "3.6 million people in Britain are gay – official"
<http://www.guardian.co.uk/uk/2005/dec/11/gayrights.immigrationpolicy> (Accessed January 2012)

Deer, Brian. "Justin Fashanu's final days"
<http://briandeer.com/justin-fashanu-1.htm> (Accessed April 2012)

Dow, Steve. "To dive for"
<http://www.stevedow.com.au/Default.aspx?id=433> (Accessed April 2012)

Evans, Martin. "Steven Davies: England cricketer announces he is gay" <http://www.telegraph.co.uk/sport/cricket/8350779/Steven-Davies-England-cricketer-announces-he-is-gay.html> (Accessed April 2012)

Flynn, Paul. "The 'gay for Thierry Henry' outpouring heralds a new openness"

<http://www.guardian.co.uk/commentisfree/2012/jan/10/go-gay-for-thierry-henry> (Accessed March 2012)

Gimmers, Mof. "Italian FA Advises Gay Players 'Don't Come Out': Damiano Tommasi Says Homosexuals Not Welcome In Changing Rooms" <http://www.anorak.co.uk/303621/sports/italian-fa-advises-gay-players-dont-come-out-damiano-tommasi-say-homosexuals-not-welcome-in-changing-rooms.html> (Accessed February 2012)

Godwin, Hugh & Harris, Nick. "Two top gay footballers stay in closet" <http://www.independent.co.uk/sport/football/news-and-comment/two-top-gay-footballers-stay-in-closet-1845787.html> (Accessed February 2012)

Hoult, Nick. "Steven Davies has full backing of England squad after announcing he is gay, says Ian Bell" <http://www.telegraph.co.uk/sport/cricket/international/england/8351718/Steven-Davies-has-full-backing-of-England-squad-after-announcing-he-is-gay-says-Ian-Bell.html> (Accessed April 2012)

Jacques, Juliet. "Justin Fashanu and the politics of memory" <http://www.newstatesman.com/blogs/lifestyle/2012/05/justin-fashanu-and-politics-memory> (Accessed May 2012)

King, Dominic. "Everton are happy to give their support to Liverpool Pride" <http://www.chesterchronicle.co.uk/chester-sport/everton-fc-news/2012/07/21/everton-are-happy-to-give-their-support-to-liverpool-pride-59067-31441523> (Accessed July 2012)

Longman, Jere. "In African Women's Soccer, Homophobia Remains an Obstacle" <http://www.nytimes.com/2011/06/23/sports/soccer/in-african-womens-soccer-homophobia-remains-an-obstacle.html> (Accessed April 2012)

Luckhurst, Samuel. "John Fashanu Claims Brother Justin Wasn't Gay – He Just Wanted Attention" <http://www.huffingtonpost.co.uk/2012/03/16/john-fashanu-doesnt-believe-his-brother-justin-was-gay_n_1353917.html> (Accessed April 2012)

Magowan, Alistair. "John Amaechi says 'reactive' FA responsible for homophobia" <http://www.bbc.co.uk/sport/0/football/17086342> (Accessed March 2012)

Ponting, Ivan. "Obituary: Justin Fashanu" <http://www.independent.co.uk/news/obituaries/obituary-justin-fashanu-1161484.html> (Accessed February 2012)

Sanusi, Leke. "Homophobia in the Nigerian Women's Football Team" <http://thinkafricapress.com/nigeria/sexual-orientation-exclusion> (Accessed May 2012)

Tatchell, Peter. "Justin Fashanu – Homophobia Destroyed Him" <http://www.petertatchell.net/sport/justin_fashanu.htm> (Accessed March 2012)

Tippetts, Adrian. "Kick homophobia out of football" <http://www.guardian.co.uk/commentisfree/2009/aug/18/homophobia-football-anti-gay-abuse-fa> (Accessed March 2012)

Tremlett, Giles. "Gay group tackles football homophobia" <http://www.guardian.co.uk/world/2009/feb/28/gay-rights-spain-football> (Accessed February 2012)

Weathers, Helen. "British Lions rugby legend Gareth Thomas: 'It's ended my marriage and nearly driven me to suicide. Now it's time to tell the world the truth – I'm gay'" <http://www.dailymail.co.uk/femail/article-1237035/British-Lions-rugby-legend-Gareth-Thomas-Its-ended-marriage-nearly-driven-suicide-Now-time-tell-world-truth--Im-gay.html> (Accessed April 2012)

White, Duncan. "Should gay footballers come out?" <http://blogs.telegraph.co.uk/sport/duncanwhite/100005418/should-gay-footballers-come-out> (Accessed April 2012)

Williams, Matt. "Is homophobia in football still a taboo?" <http://news.bbc.co.uk/sport1/hi/football/4426278.stm> (Accessed April 2012)

Winter, Henry. "Memories of Justin" <http://www.thejustincampaign.com/henry_winter.htm> (Accessed March 2012)

Zeigler Jr., Cyd. "David Test, American pro soccer player, comes out as gay, regrets not doing it earlier" <http://outsports.com/jocktalkblog/2011/11/10/david-testo-american-professional-soccer-player-comes-out> (Accessed May 2012)

Zeigler Jr., Cyd. "Out athlete tells others to stay in the closet" <http://outsports.com/jocktalkblog/2011/02/01/german-goalkeeper-ursula-holl-tells-athletes-to-stay-in-the-closet> (Accessed May 2012)

Australian Independent. "Gay footballers debate intensifies after 'ballet' quote" <http://austrianindependent.com/news/Sports/2010-11-17/5351/Gay_footballers_debate_intensifies_after_'ballet'_quote> (Accessed February 2012)

BBC News. "Fashanu: a rising star who faded too soon" <http://news.bbc.co.uk/1/hi/uk/87288.stm> (Accessed February 2012)

BBC News. "Football 'failing on homophobia'" <http://news.bbc.co.uk/1/hi/uk/8197306.stm> (Accessed February 2012)

BBC News. "Gay football lovers on the game" <http://news.bbc.co.uk/1/hi/uk/8197891.stm> (Accessed March 2012)

BBC News. "Liverpool Football Club join Pride parade" <http://www.bbc.co.uk/news/uk-england-merseyside-18779803> (Accessed July 2012)

BBC News Magazine. "Why are there no openly gay footballers?" <http://news.bbc.co.uk/1/hi/4427718.stm> (Accessed March 2012)

BBC Sport. "Ex-Lion Gareth Thomas reveals he is gay" <http://news.bbc.co.uk/sport1/hi/rugby_union/welsh/8421956.stm> (Accessed April 2012)

BBC Sport. "Fifa boss Sepp Blatter sparks Qatar gay controversy" <http://news.bbc.co.uk/sport1/hi/football/9284186.stm> (Accessed February 2012)

BBC Sport. "In-depth interview – Gareth Thomas" <http://news.bbc.co.uk/sport1/hi/rugby_union/welsh/8425335.stm> (Accessed April 2012)

Der Kapitan. "Bilde.de: New Excerpts From Lahm's Book. Part IV" <http://derkapitan.wordpress.com/2011/08/28/bild-de-new-excerpts-from-lahms-book-part-iv> (Accessed January 2012)

Football Italia. "Serie A divided on 'coming out'" <http://www.football-italia.net/18360/serie-stars-divided-coming-out> (Accessed May 2012)

Independent on Sunday. "The IOS Pink List 2010" <http://www.independent.co.uk/news/people/news/the-iiosi-pink-list-2010-2040472.html> (Accessed April 2012)

Mail Online. "Four Tottenham fans banned over indecent Campbell chants" <http://www.dailymail.co.uk/sport/football/article-1123823/Four-Tottenham-fans-banned-indecent-Campbell-chants.html> (Accessed February 2012)

Mail Online. "Scholes in storm over 'poof' outburst" <http://www.dailymail.co.uk/sport/football/article-407317/Scholes-storm-poof-outburst.html> (Accessed March 2012)

Mail Online. "Tottenham supporters guilty of 'disgusting' homophobic football chants aimed at Sol Campbell" <http://www.dailymail.co.uk/news/article-1182848/Tottenham-supporters-guilty-disgusting-homophobic-football-chants-aimed-Sol-Campbell.html> (Accessed February 2012)

Pink News. "Ashley Cole files lawsuit over gay orgy story" <http://www.pinknews.co.uk/2006/03/03/ashley-cole-files-lawsuit-over-gay-orgy-story> (Accessed April 2012)

Pink News. "FIFA President: Homosexuality more popular in women's football" <http://www.pinknews.co.uk/2008/03/07/fifa-president-homosexuality-more-popular-in-womens-football> (Accessed May 2012)

Pink News. "Freddie Ljungberg 'proud' of gay gossip" <http://www.pinknews.co.uk/2010/06/15/freddie-ljungberg-proud-of-gay-gossip> (Accessed April 2012)

Red Card Homophobia. "Homosexuality and Women's Football" <http://redcardhomophobia.wordpress.com/2011/07/25/homosexuality-and-womens-football> (Accessed May 2012)

Tackle. "Fashanu: The First"
<http://tacklemedia.blogspot.co.uk/2011/12/fashanu-first.html>
(Accessed March 2012)

The Australian. "The 'responsibility' of gay athletes"
<http://www.theaustralian.com.au/news/features/the-responsibility-of-gay-athletes/story-e6frg8h6-1226006836102> (Accessed April 2012)

The Local. "Goalie Angerer reveals she is bisexual"
<http://www.thelocal.de/sport/20101202-31557.html> (Accessed May 2012)

The Secret Footballer. "Fans stop gay footballers from coming out"
<http://www.guardian.co.uk/football/blog/2011/mar/12/the-secret-footballer-gay-players> (Accessed March 2012)

The Sun. "Macheda 'n Nile in gay slur rap"
<http://www.thesun.co.uk/sol/homepage/sport/football/4158531/Twitter-news-Federico-Macheda-and-Nile-Ranger-charged-with-making-a-Twitter-slur.html> (Accessed April 2012)

The Sun. "Ravel's 7k fine for Twitter rant"
<http://www.thesun.co.uk/sol/homepage/sport/football/4147334/Ravel-Morrisons-7k-fine-for-Twitter-rant.html> (Accessed April 2012)

The Telegraph. "Five trailblazing gay sportsmen"
<http://www.telegraph.co.uk/news/worldnews/europe/germany/8524212/Five-trailblazing-gay-sportsmen.html> (Accessed March 2012)

This Is Nottingham. "Nottingham Forest legend Viv Anderson: Brian Clough transformed my career"
<http://www.thisisnottingham.co.uk/Anderson-Clough-transformed-career/story-12244647-detail/story.html> (Accessed March 2012)

Printed in Great Britain
by Amazon.co.uk, Ltd.,
Marston Gate.